# Against the Wind

# Against the Wind

## Leadership at 36,000 Feet

Donya Ball

ROWMAN & LITTLEFIELD
*Lanham • Boulder • New York • London*

Published by Rowman & Littlefield
An imprint of The Rowman & Littlefield Publishing Group, Inc.
4501 Forbes Boulevard, Suite 200, Lanham, Maryland 20706
www.rowman.com

86-90 Paul Street, London EC2A 4NE

Copyright © 2024 by Donya Ball

*All rights reserved.* No part of this book may be reproduced in any form or by any electronic or mechanical means, including information storage and retrieval systems, without written permission from the publisher, except by a reviewer who may quote passages in a review.

British Library Cataloguing in Publication Information Available

**Library of Congress Cataloging-in-Publication Data**

Names: Ball, Donya, 1978– author.
Title: Against the wind : leadership at 36,000 feet / Donya Ball.
Description: Lanham, Maryland : Roman & Littlefield Publishing Group, 2024. |
 Includes bibliographical references.
Identifiers: LCCN 2023041233 (print) | LCCN 2023041234 (ebook) |
 ISBN 9781475870794 (cloth) | ISBN 9781475870800 (paperback) |
 ISBN 9781475870817 (ebook)
Subjects: LCSH: School management and organization—United States. | School
 administrators—United States. | Educational leadership—United States.
Classification: LCC LB2801.A2 B353 2024 (print) | LCC LB2801.A2 (ebook) |
 DDC 371.200973—dc23/eng/20230906
LC record available at https://lccn.loc.gov/2023041233
LC ebook record available at https://lccn.loc.gov/2023041234

*For Angie,
the wind beneath my wings.*

*For Renée and Diane,
the first ones that guided me to
safe landing through rough air.*

*For "Powerhouse,"
Heather, Melanie, Yolanda, and Laura,
the ultimate flight crew.*

# Contents

| | |
|---|---|
| Foreword | ix |
| Preface | xi |
| Introduction | xv |

### PART 1: PREFLIGHT CHECKLIST — 1

1. The Flight Crew: Creating Your Support System — 3
2. Dynamic Balance: Equilibrium in Life and Leadership — 11
3. Security Screening for Hijackers: Avoiding Time Mismanagement and Micromanaging — 23

### PART 2: EN-ROUTE — 35

4. Reading Your Instruments: Charisma, Clarity, and Communication — 37
5. Inflow and Outflow: Hiring and Firing with Dignity — 51
6. Wind Currents: The Push and Pull of Competing Agendas — 59

### PART 3: VICTORY AFTER DISASTER — 73

7. Scanning the Horizon: Recognizing Early Warning Signs — 75
8. Emergency Landing: Character Under Fire — 87
9. The Crash: Navigating Career Setbacks — 95
10. The Rubble: Finding Meaning in the Mayhem — 105

**PART 4: JOURNEY'S END** **117**

11  Taking Flight Again: Discovering New Purpose 119

12  The Destination: Sustainable Leadership 129

Bibliography 143

About the Author 147

# Foreword

When leaders ascend to top positions, why do so many of them crash and burn? As someone who has worked in leadership positions for many years, I have seen firsthand the impact that stress, burnout, and fatigue can have on leaders. It affects their ability to inspire and manage teams effectively. Yet despite leaders' search for answers and solutions, the qualities of a successful leader often remain elusive.

This is why Dr. Ball's book is so important.

Dr. Ball unpacks the complex and multifaceted concept of leadership in a clear, accessible way that will resonate with leaders of all ages and stages. Her book is insightful and deeply relatable. Her approachable and engaging writing style will appeal to both veteran executives and emerging leaders.

Through practical advice, understandable analogies, and personal stories from expert leaders, Dr. Ball helps readers cultivate important leadership skills. Her content is steeped in applied research and the deep expertise of seasoned leaders. From the practical self-assessments to the captivating flight analogies, *Against the Wind: Leadership at 36,000 Feet* is a valuable resource for anyone looking to become a more effective leader.

Many leaders forget that personal growth is a crucial part of their toolkit. They overlook the fact that emotional intelligence is the key to managing their ever-changing environment. In her relatable and research-filled book, Dr. Ball emphasizes both the inner and outer aspects of leadership. She demonstrates that the most successful leaders take time to cultivate self-awareness, empathy, resilience, and compassion.

Dr. Ball shows how to lead from a place of authenticity and vulnerability. She recognizes that successful leadership requires not only the ability to manage and inspire others but also the capacity to manage one's own emotions, biases, and habits.

In this timely and insightful book, Dr. Ball provides readers with an accessible and engaging flight plan for developing the skills, insights, and character needed for the ever-changing conditions surrounding leadership. She shows how proficient leaders can transform not only individual leaders in their care but entire organizations.

Whether you are a superintendent, CEO, or new team leader, I encourage you to read and digest the contents of this book with an open mind and an open heart. I have no doubt that it will inspire and assist you in your journey towards becoming the courageous and impactful leader you strive to be.

Debb Oliver, EdD<br>
COO of the Consortium of State School Boards Associations<br>
Co-founder of Mindful SEAD

# Preface

*"When everything seems to be going against you, remember that the airplane takes off against the wind, not with it."*

—Henry Ford

Before we take flight, find your favorite decompression spot and pour yourself an even bigger glass of your favorite beverage. Or perhaps an even stronger drink. You pick.

Get ready for another dose of wise guidance and stories from a powerful group of seasoned leaders out in the field. These are the two ingredients that make this series different.

Leaders want key foundational leadership principles. They want a map, a compass, and a guide to help them navigate the challenges of being a hated leader, facilitating engaging and fierce conversations, overcoming career disappointment, and creating a positive brand for the watching world. That's exactly what the first book in this series, *Adjusting the Sails,* provided. It introduced crucial leadership concepts that I have discovered as I have served in a variety of leadership positions.

Experienced leaders must have a strong foundation that helps them gauge their future path. This foundation serves as a compass for making high-leverage decisions that can have a profound impact on the organization and its people. It is critical to have a map, a guide, and an instruction manual for the future. That is what *Against the Wind* will provide, as it builds on the concepts introduced in *Adjusting the Sails.*

However, a map is not all we need. Seasoned executives also need other leaders to relate to and discuss challenges with. They need compassionate, listening ears to empathize as they face their ever-increasing responsibilities. With every career ladder climb, they need fellow leaders who understand.

*Against the Wind* will continue to provide the real-life voices and stories from leaders that you have grown to expect.

When the first book in this leadership series was published, the feedback began to pour in. Leaders appreciated the wise advice and key principles. But even more, they appreciated the camaraderie the book provided as they went through critical leadership challenges. *Adjusting the Sails* was grounded in down-to-earth storytelling and real-life leadership lessons from the field, and the feedback has been consistent. As I spoke to executives who had read the first book in the series, one point surfaced over and over: *We want more. We want more raw stories. We want more conversations. We want more practical, no-nonsense, real talk.*

That's why book two of the series, *Against the Wind*, has brought in even more voices. Even more stories. Even more camaraderie. While researching for this book, I interviewed several leaders, both in and out of the educational field. They each contributed their wise insights. But most of all, they contributed their down-to-earth stories that will encourage, challenge, and refresh you.

Let me explain a bit more about my passion for wise guidance and practical stories.

I'm passionate about sharing elevated wisdom for leaders. In *Adjusting the Sails*, I shared concepts that are absolutely essential to starting a successful leadership career. These ideas and skills have proven true for me in my own experiences, and they have proven true for other leaders in weathering the trials and tribulations of leadership. However, they are base camp leadership skills.

In *Against the Wind*, it is time to level up. It is time to fasten your seatbelts and prepare to take off against the wind, elevating your career to a deeper and more sustainable journey that will last for the long term. While *Adjusting the Sails* was written for aspiring and entry-level leadership, *Against the Wind* focuses on the turbulence that middle and advanced leadership require. It expands on the foundational principles presented in the first book by adding new stories, new lessons, and a higher degree of implementation.

I'm passionate about elevated storytelling. Leaders who read *Adjusting the Sails* voiced their overwhelming appreciation for the real talk, the conversations, and the storytelling. *Against the Wind* will continue with the strategy that makes this leadership series stand out. It will include fewer stats and over-the-top studies, and instead focus more on down-to-earth guidance. And let's not forget the lessons learned from highly successful and influential leaders both in the field of education and beyond.

Whether you are a new leader who is thinking about the next career move or you are an experienced leader who continues to learn and grow, you need to hear the candid, real, and honest viewpoints of other leaders. You need stories of the daily struggles and triumphs of what really happens behind the scenes in offices and out in the field. And that is exactly what this book provides.

Stories have power. Whenever I attend professional development events and conferences, there is typically one session that I look forward to the most. It is not typically the keynote, general, or breakout sessions. It is the post-conference session, where leaders get together and share real-life stories.

Don't get me wrong. As a speaker myself, I absolutely know the power of a great keynote that leaves the crowd feeling inspired, energized, and ready to take on new leadership challenges. But what most of us leaders really yearn for is to know we are not going through this wild adventure alone. That's why I absolutely love dining with friends, sharing a beverage with colleagues, or taking a walk around the hotel block with new acquaintances. The power is in the stories that we tell each other—the "misery loves company" effect.

As you read this book, you will feel like you're in a front-row seat, listening in on personal conversations with leaders from all around the globe. They will share their stories of growth, tragedy, and triumph. They will impart the wisdom they've gained over a lifetime. And as you continue to be charged with making major decisions that not only impact the people you serve but also your local communities and often global society, they will speak the words you most need to hear: "You are not alone."

Although this book is written through the lens of education administration because of my personal experiences, all public and private sector leaders can relate to the lessons and principles shared in this book.

As you embrace your next career move, give yourself a few minutes to reflect on the elevated wisdom and elevated storytelling found in *Against the Wind*. It is time to give yourself the tools you need to travel to your next destination. Fasten your seatbelt and prepare for takeoff with an open mind. Stop for a moment to reflect on your current leadership realities and where you want to go and grow.

As all the leaders in this book can attest, leadership isn't easy. In fact, it often feels like being on a jet plane approaching an unexpected storm system. These types of challenges can leave even the most skilled pilot with an elevated heart rate and sweaty hands. The stories in this book don't shy away from the brutal realities of leadership, but they also show that leaders can survive the difficulties. Just as the infrastructure of the plane can withstand the eye of the storm, so can you. Let's raise our glasses to that.

# Introduction

Now that we are one beverage in, it's time to refill your glass, take a deep breath, and give yourself the time to think about how far you have come.

Taking the plunge into your first leadership position is one thing, but promotion is another ball game. It's worth recognizing and celebrating. Perhaps your new position was the result of mentors and coaches singing your praises, giving you the push to try this thing called leadership. Or perhaps it was just a natural progression of upward promotions.

Either way, you are probably asking yourself how to best equip yourself for whatever lies ahead. You are wondering what the common challenges are that leaders will continue to experience as they forge forward in their careers. You wonder how you can ensure a solid level of sanity along the way.

In this book, you will learn from the incredible leaders who have been there and done that. You will learn their tips for launching your higher-level career, spotting potential problems, weathering the inevitable storms, and enjoying every small destination along the way.

The book is organized into four parts: a pre-flight checklist to set the conditions of a successful career, en route assurances to keep your leadership career progressing smoothly, crisis measures for the inevitable disasters of life, and wisdom for crafting a destination that truly brings satisfaction.

In Part 1, Preflight Checklist, you will learn the absolutely critical conditions that must be in place in order for an experienced leader to make it through the rough air. Without the preflight analysis, you can forget about embarking on the journey. In this section, you will learn:

- The importance of building a flight crew—people that serve as your support system throughout every small and long journey.

- How to ensure you have the correct balance and mental conditions for success, both in your day job and home job.
- How to make sure that you have "security measures" in place that will help you avoid dangerous mentalities that will hijack your success.

Each of these tools must be in place before you can even take flight as a top-tier leader.

In Part 2, En-Route, we will transition to the leadership skills you will need to make your flight as smooth as possible. You'll learn how to read a room like a pilot reads his instruments, becoming an expert at understanding any audience you are confronted with. You then examine the critical leadership skills of hiring and firing, as well as working with the constant push and pull of competing agendas. These tools will help you survive a long career in leadership.

In Part 3, Victory After Disaster, we will dive into some of the most relatable and encouraging content of all: how to survive in case of emergency. As licensed pilot Stan Greenspan said, "Flying lessons are not so much about flying but about emergencies. You can't 'pull over' and deal with something on a cloud someplace. You need to be aware at all times of someplace to put the plane down if you really need to."[1] The same is true of leadership. The higher you go in leadership, the more prepared you need to be for disaster.

In this section, you'll learn preventative strategies that will prepare you for whatever comes your way. You'll learn to build the character you need for the inevitable emergencies as well as strategies to navigate career setbacks. You'll find out how to pick up the pieces and recover from career rejection.

In Part 4, Journey's End, you'll learn to take flight again. You'll hear inspiring stories of leaders who have found new and uncharted territories for their life and leadership. You'll learn that although leadership positions are extremely difficult, they can lead to beautiful things you've never imagined. And you'll hear reflections from seasoned leaders about how you can enjoy the destination—even during the pit stops along the way.

Each chapter contains a flight-related metaphor that brings the leadership principles to life. At the end of each chapter, a summary called Air Traffic Control wraps up the concept with practical steps and proven processes that will help every high-level leader overcome even the greatest of flight disturbances. Just like the air-traffic control tower provides reliable guidance for an aircraft, these sections give wise communication to guide you from your current conditions toward calmer skies.

This book will serve as your aeronautical map as you continue to embark into the challenging leadership world for which there is often no GPS. These strategic approaches will help you handle the wildest of rough air. Relatable stories and down-to-earth guidance will help you prepare for takeoff against the wind. Together, we will survive the ever-changing leadership conditions while up in the air. Let's prepare for departure!

**NOTE**

1. "How Much of a Pilot's Training Is Emergency Landing Practices?," last modified March 20, 2017. Accessed November 30, 2022, https://slate.com/human-interest/2017/03/how-much-of-a-pilots-training-is-emergency-landing-practices.html.

*Part 1*

# PREFLIGHT CHECKLIST

## Chapter 1

# The Flight Crew

## *Creating Your Support System*

It's been one of those days. You had to make a difficult leadership decision, and now everyone seems to be turning against you. As you sit alone in your office at the end of the day, you shake your head. The sun is setting, and you're wondering how you can go on. You put your head in your hands and groan.

*Is this even worth it?*

Enter your flight crew. Your phone pings, and you remember that today is the day you meet your support group of fellow leadership BFFs at the neighborhood bar and grill. You leap into your car. You feel like you can't get there fast enough. Seated with your group of fellow leaders fifteen minutes later, you let off your pent-up frustration. You tell the story of the person you fired, the leadership decision you made, or the pivot you initiated. You provide context and explain why you made your difficult decision. Then you kick back, and your flight crew takes over.

Your support team does a lot of listening and not a lot of talking. They truly take it all in. They provide empathy, kindness, and support. At the end of the day, their goal is to provide you with some much-needed guidance that is based on sound reasoning. After your support team has offered their comfort and ideas, you can tangibly feel the lightness in your chest. You feel better.

Whether you're an introvert, an extrovert, or anything in between, having a support system made up of your closest friends is critical. Having people to whom you can vent after a crazy day is often the only thing that will get you to the other side of survival in leadership.

In every facet of leadership, there are times when leaders and executives have to make unpopular decisions. They have to lead the way and work through adversity with the people they serve. Leaders have to carry out what they believe is right, even when others are not in favor. It is a strategy that happens throughout a leader's career. You know the direction you need to go in your decision-making as leaders, but it is not necessarily a popular choice or what is supported. You absolutely need your support system for those days when you have to make a difficult decision.

Adjusting to your unpopular position will happen more efficiently when you have a strong support system ready to catch you during times of despair. Sometimes, it just seems like the world is against you. When just one hater makes it their mission to bring you down, it is amazing how that one person can feel like a thousand haters.

The stress that this one person imposes on your mental well-being most often feels like too much to bear. It is during these times that every leader needs their flight crew ready to gather the troops, get together, and problem-solve. They will help you navigate the difficult task of mitigating the damage that the hater has caused. Often, that damage is too difficult to repair alone. You need your flight crew to aggressively come together with a plan of action, ready to help out a sister or brother in need.

Bryson Daniel, a seasoned army armor and cavalryman with more than thirty years of service operating, leading, teaching, and planning at some notable sites like the National Training Center in Fort Irwin, California; Iraq; Afghanistan; the Pentagon and Army Futures Command, shares some important lessons he learned about support systems.[1]

When he was a lieutenant colonel in charge of the Combined Arms Battalion in the First Armored Division in Fort Bliss, Texas, he used to take his team to do long field problems. They'd been trained using simulated battles and engagements with other units. These would go on for weeks at a time. Historically, they would end on Friday evenings. The troops would be so excited to see their families that they would start making shortcuts. Exhausted, they just wanted to get home.

During one of these mock battles, Bryson made an unpopular decision. Instead of sending his troops home on Friday in a hurried state, he made the decision to take his time and deploy back on Saturday morning. He did not want his team to lose their successes and all the great things they had done in the field.

This made Lieutenant Daniel hugely unpopular. He got pushback from the soldiers as well as from their husbands or wives. Every army comes with an army of families with it, and those families can voice strong disagreement when a leader makes an unpopular decision.

That's when it's critical to have a support team. Bryson engaged his fellow leaders on his support team. He said, "How can we get in front of this discontentment?" His support team helped him make a plan to invite the men's families for a BBQ dinner the night before they went into the field, which served both agendas. It allowed the families to connect after a long time away and allowed the unit to continue to make good decisions by being decoupled from a rushed timeline.

The soldiers would get an additional chance to get out of the field, and their families would get the opportunity to meet out in the desert. Instead of rushing in, partying in exhaustion, and making shortcuts and problems, they waited an extra day. As a result, Bryson's unit was considered a disciplined unit.

Can you relate? When the time comes to make an unpopular decision, you won't be able to thrive without the support, encouragement, and ideas that your team can provide.

How does a support team play out in real life? Let's look at how a group of school superintendents in the Central Valley region of California implemented their unique support team for maximum benefit. These leaders got together to form a special and important relational support group. They named themselves "Powerhouse."

The five women in this group are all very different. Every leader is wildly unique in personality and position. Yet they each provide a needed perspective to the group. But the camaraderie that they provide each other is absolutely essential.

Let's look closely at each person's unique contribution.

- Katherine is a rock-solid, seasoned district leader. She has a heart of gold for the people that she serves. Highly respected, she has earned a mass amount of respect throughout the years. Because of her proven track record, she now mentors several aspiring and current district leaders. She contributes coaching and guidance to help others be the best leaders they can be.
- Isabel is a relatively new superintendent, but she has already faced incredible challenges. Her split board has not always been the most supportive, yet she is driven and 100 percent committed to having a successful career as a superintendent. Prior to her district leadership position, Isabel served as an instructional consultant, traveling throughout the state and country delivering high-quality professional development and training. She serves an extremely diverse community.
- Taylor lights up every room she enters with her bubbly personality. She is a fierce and passionate leader who has served in a variety of teaching and administrative positions and is currently the superintendent of a single school district, a small K–8 school in the heart of California. Taylor enjoys life outside of work, and her creative, upbeat personality is contagious.
- Gianna has taught the group the most life lessons. She has had to balance some major personal life challenges with a highly demanding career as superintendent of a small K–8 school. Gianna has not had it easy the past few years. In fact, she is the poster woman for resilience and how to

overcome some major life challenges that one could never predict. Gianna strives for high academic achievement, and her staff absolutely knows through her constant messaging that students will continuously improve from one year to the next.
- Alexis is a superintendent of two TK–8 charter schools, faculty at a local university, author, and speaker. She is constantly setting new personal and professional goals, so slowing down for her is not really an option. Alexis travels a ton for pleasure to offset the high demands of work stressors.

What do all five of these women have in common? They are all superintendents and moms. Other than that, they have very little in common. They serve in five very different educational settings with very different challenges. They have extremely different and diverse backgrounds, making them all extremely unique. And yet they come together over their favorite beverage and laugh and talk about everything from personal to professional lives.

Practically, their get-together sessions consist of several key ingredients. First and foremost, laughter is a nonnegotiable part of these meetings. They talk about everything under the sun. They discuss serious topics, like the local leader who seems to be causing some major waves in the community. They also talk about everyday joys and sorrows. Or they gush over how good the margaritas taste at the local Mexican restaurant.

These women have a deep admiration for each other. Without a doubt, all five members of Powerhouse know that they have each other's back. They know where to find answers, and they know where to find a listening ear. It is truly this relationship that these leaders rely on to get them through their day-in and day-out craziness as leaders.

What would these women do without each other? They truly have become a family. During the week, they are more than ready to reach out to each other through group texts when a pressing matter is at hand.

These women could not ever imagine moving through the motions of leadership without each other. But because they have a strong support team, they wake up each day ready to tackle whatever roadblock is placed in front of them.

Every airplane has a flight crew that helps to operate the airplane while in flight. The captain calls the shots and organizes the entire adventure. The first officer sits beside the captain, ready to assist in any way necessary. The second and third officers offer the pilot a break during long flights, and the relief crew serves the same role.

Historically, the flight engineer helped maintain the engine, the airborne sensor operator kept track of where the airplane was in space, the navigator kept the plane on the right path, and the radio operator handled communication.[2] Each member of the support team is vital for the captain's success.

No one expects the pilot to rely on the passengers for support. Not even the flight attendants can provide this type of relief, support, and encouragement to the pilot. Instead, the pilot needs the aircrew to weather the storms and the long distances in flight. These are the support people that allow them to serve the passengers.

In the same way, it's impossible to expect your clients, your coworkers, or your subordinates to truly provide the support you need. Even spouses, adult children, and other relatives are limited in what they can do as our off-hours support people.

While they are vital to our success, they can only help us to a certain extent. Although our family likely has our absolute best interests in mind, they do not necessarily have similar education, leadership experiences, and like-minded strategy-building that the flight crew exhibits. This is not to say that those closest to us and related to us can't serve as an important sounding board after a long day. It is just that the flight crew has a unique and special skill set to be equipped to offer sound advice and guidance.

That's why you need an off-hours support team—a flight crew—that can offer relief, refreshment, and a listening ear when you are losing energy on a long flight. Your off-hours support team can assist you in ways that are very different from the camaraderie you receive from the people you work with in your office or organization.

What are those differences? It's very simple: the relationship. Certain healthy boundaries must be set and respected when it comes to the relationships with the people within your company, business, or organization. Quite frankly, as an organizational leader, you must maintain a certain amount of composure and steadfast professionalism among your staff. However, your off-hours flight crew—that is where the real magic happens. These are the people that you can spill the beans with, discuss hot topics that could be highly offensive to others, and, best of all, let off steam.

When a leader does not have a good off-hours support team, they often feel tempted to cross professional boundaries with subordinates just to let off steam. Many leaders have to travel for work and attend dinners. As the drinks start flowing, the conversation can easily go from professional in nature to extremely lighthearted. There is nothing worse than watching a top-level professional consume too many drinks on an empty stomach, stumbling over his words as he makes an absolute fool of himself.

Yes, some would say that's what out-of-town shenanigans are for. Everyone needs to be able to let loose among safe company once in a while, right? But the question must be asked: How much is too much? What is crossing the line?

It is safe to say that there is definitely a professional expectation of decorum, even among work colleagues. When attending a professional career-oriented event, whether local or beyond, you have to be mindful of boundaries—especially when you, as the leader, are around those that you are supervising.

However, it's different with your flight crew. It's different because they typically do not have an agenda or motive to see you fail. Your flight crew wants to see you be the most successful leader that you can be. Your flight crew members are your biggest cheerleaders.

Because your flight crew plays such an important role in your life, it is critical to choose your flight crew wisely. How does one go about solidifying their flight crew? There are two parts to this important task.

## WHO SHOULD BE A PART OF MY SUPPORT TEAM?

First, we must solidify the "who." The relationships formed must be authentic in nature. In other words, these are not forced relationships. Instead, you must form a support system with people who truly enjoy each other's company and definitely want and look forward to the next get-together.

True, there's a big challenge here: authentic relationships take time. Sometimes, you will meet these people, and the bond happens relatively quickly and easily. But other times, it takes some strategy to seek out your solid off-hours support system.

With the insane number of hours that a leader works in a day, how is it possible to also form authentic relationships and make friends that become your A team? Even though it's a challenge, you must make this an utmost priority.

When accepting people into your inner circle, there is a certain amount of strategy to focus on. You shouldn't pick just anyone. Pick trustworthy, experienced, and wise individuals who are like-minded and work a similar job. These people are charged with continuously challenging you.

You do not want your flight crew to be people who are going to steer you in the wrong direction when the going gets tough. When determining exactly who will serve as your off-hours support team, pick authentic, wise individuals who truly value you as a person.

Our off-hours support and flight crew should absolutely consist of a professional psychologist, marriage and family therapist, or a life coach as well. Bryson discussed the importance of seeking professional help to recover from trauma such as PTSD, and this is a critical step. No leader should ever put professional success over personal healing.

Coaches, psychologists, and therapists offer a listening ear, wise advice, and total confidentiality that our subordinates cannot offer. A therapist's office is an excellent place to vent after a difficult day. They will help you reach your full potential as a leader.

So many leaders grew up in an era when seeking outside professional therapy was looked at as weak and unnecessary. However, these professionals are trained and understand the right questions to ask to truly get at the root cause of the stress. They can help you uncover the root of the insane amount of pressure you are feeling that is depleting your core physical and emotional well-being.

Leaders need to normalize and model the fact that seeking outside help is a healthy action, providing a much-needed perspective. When leaders discourage or talk negatively about these professionals, they get themselves into predicaments. They also promote an unhealthy culture where employees keep their problems to themselves, not wanting to be perceived as weak. Instead, you, as a leader, can make the first move by modeling healthy habits for your employees.

## HOW SHOULD I BUILD MY SUPPORT TEAM?

Second, let's talk about the "how." Once your support group is formed, how do you offer the best support to these people you genuinely care about? When you hear a problem come up, the worst thing that you can do is rush to give advice and guidance.

Otherwise, you will put your fellow leader in an even bigger predicament than when he or she arrived at the get-together. Instead of slapping a superficial bandage on a gaping wound, offer empathy and depth. Rely on your own wrong leadership experiences in order to provide perspective.

As a part of the flight crew, your job is not necessarily to direct your fellow leaders to where they want to go. You don't need to counsel them to stay within their comfort levels. It is very healthy for your support system to help each other see the other side of an issue and to play devil's advocate.

The last thing a leader wants is to move forward rashly into a decision that will negatively impact his or her future career. Each member of the flight crew can serve as a coach, a mentor, and a friend to the others in the group. How fortunate is the leader who has a solid off-hours support team to call upon during times of intense trials and stressful heartbreaks?

## AIR TRAFFIC CONTROL

The preflight check includes making sure your flight crew is on board and prepared. Before you take flight on your next-level leadership position, you need to make sure your support team is in place. Like the flight crew in an airplane, you need a solid support system to help you through the rough patches in leadership.

- Support teams offer types of help and advice that a colleague, subordinate, or family member cannot easily offer.
- A therapist, life coach, or psychologist can be an important member of your support system.
- Choose authentic friends who have similar leadership positions but are not a part of your organization.
- Choose people who will offer you the wisdom you need to hear, not the platitudes you want to hear.

## NOTES

1. Retired colonel, in discussion with the author, August 12, 2022. Name changed for privacy.

2. "Aircrew," Wikipedia. Accessed September 19, 2022, https://en.wikipedia.org/wiki/Aircrew.

*Chapter 2*

# Dynamic Balance

*Equilibrium in Life and Leadership*

In May 2018, a Boeing 737 went down in a cassava field in Cuba, taking the lives of more than one hundred people. Twenty of them were pastors on their way back from a retreat. The accident was called "the deadliest aviation accident in Cuba in three decades."[1] For two months, no one knew what had gone wrong.[2]

Then it was discovered: There had been errors in the weight and balance calculations. Before takeoff on every flight, pilots are required to calculate the center of gravity of their airplanes. If the plane has a heavier load in the rear, the pilot needs to compensate with extra balance on the front of the plane. If there is more pressure on the front of the aircraft, the pilot needs to compensate in the back.

A pilot can't just calculate the balance one time and use the same results every time he takes a trip. Why? Because flying is a dynamic process: each time a pilot flies, the balance shifts. Depending on the way the aircraft is loaded from front to back, the center of gravity changes. When pilots ignore the importance of weight and balance, devastating consequences can occur.

## DISASTROUS CONSEQUENCES

In October 2006, another pilot failed to pay close attention to the center of gravity calculations before he took off.[3] Like many pilots, he rushed through the calculations, not taking them seriously.[4] Unable to lift off the ground because of the hurried computations, the aircraft zoomed off the end of the runway, rammed through a fence, crashed into cars on a six-lane highway, smashed into a building, and burst into flames.[5] The crash would have been easily avoidable if the pilot had paid attention to this basic area of pre-flight preparation.[6]

Reflecting on this incident, NTSB Chairman Mark Rosenker reflected, "When it comes to transportation safety, *there are no shortcuts.*"[7]

The same is true for leaders. When it comes to balancing life and leadership, there are no shortcuts. Just like an "improperly loaded aircraft" can cause "loss of life and destruction of valuable equipment,"[8] an improperly balanced life means we can lose valuable parts of our lives. Just like an unbalanced airplane can keep a flight from reaching its destination or from taking off in the first place, a lack of leadership balance can mean that we fail to take flight in leadership or that we fail to get where we want to go. As we calculate the situation-specific balance of life and leadership, there truly are no shortcuts.

Yet many leaders try to take the easy way out. They don't pay close enough attention to the balance that needs to occur between work and life. They make hasty decisions, failing to attend to the ever-changing conditions. They create a one-size-fits-all approach to balancing their professional and personal life, without realizing that the pressures in each area are constantly shifting.

It is no secret: leadership is challenging. You are stretched thin. You have a lot of late work nights and weekend work that can take away time from family and personal events. The more seasoned you become in your leadership career, the more hours you spend burning both ends. At the same time, you are tempted to rely less and less on colleagues for collaboration and help.

You start your routine with the morning cup of coffee (or three), then jump into the rat race of chaos, with little time for physical or emotional nourishment. This often results in a whole lot of heartache and burnout. People notice. Your family notices. And you just keep on going through the motions.

Leaders are balancing so much. It's a circus. It can be a difficult balancing act with kids of various ages. Sometimes we, as leaders, drop balls and forget to take care of ourselves as we tend to our children, careers, and clients. It's easy for a leader to lose himself or herself through that process.

First, you start losing your communication tools, your decision-making skills, and your character. Then you start losing pieces of your health. You don't sleep well enough because you're stressed out about the job. You don't know how to get out of the job each day so you can recover. When you enter into an executive position, you may begin to lose yourself even more.

You can feel it. You are losing your mind. Your weight may be skyrocketing or dropping like crazy, depending on how your appetite deals with stress. You are putting out fires from sun up to sun down. You are in need of major relief. Let's call this phase what it truly is. Burn Out.

For some, it takes years to recognize, "Wow, I really have let myself go and I need to get back on track." Unfortunately, it's all too common for leaders to wait until burnout sets in to take action. Do not let this happen to you. Just as you are acutely aware of the needs of the organization, you must be acutely aware of the needs of your soul for your own mental and physical survival.

How do you focus on your needs and mental health while maintaining a very high-stress career? This is where balance checkpoints come in. Just like pilots check the plane's load and balance every single time they take off, you need to have strategic checkpoints where you adjust your workload to address unbalanced stressor points *before* you burn out.

## A DYNAMIC PROCESS

Leadership calls for careful attention. Every day, the pressures of leadership are changing, subtly or not-so-subtly. Just like a pilot must pay attention to shifting weight distribution, a leader must constantly shift the balance of home, work, and personal life, depending on the amount of strain or stress coming from that area in the moment. A leader can't just make a one-time decision about how to balance personal and career needs. These needs are in constant flux and require ongoing attention.

Your moment-by-moment emotional and personal capacity, the circumstances at the office and at home, and the needs of your family and staff are constantly changing. That's why it's important to pay close attention to the way you need to adjust the balance and weight distribution of family, personal, work, and career. If you go on autopilot, ignoring the changes, there might be an avoidable disaster.

We often hear that the work-life balance is 50/50. But that's not always accurate. The balance needs to be flexible and dynamic, changing in response to fluctuating circumstances. A pilot has to check their aircraft before every flight to calculate the balance for *this* flight and how the weight is distributed *on this particular day*.

In the same way, leaders have to acknowledge that some weeks are 80 percent work and 20 percent personal, and other weeks are a little more balanced. If a staff crisis situation requires extra energy and time, your family might need to flex a bit. On the other hand, if a family member is in the hospital or in need of your support, your employees might need to pick up the slack for a while.

How do you know when you are out of balance, and what practical steps can you take to get back in check? Natalie, an admirable top-level executive, will guide us on the journey of balance. She will share what she has learned as an executive in the automotive industry, a very demanding and time-consuming industry. As educational leaders, we can learn a lot from top-level executives in other high-stress fields. As a wife and mother, Natalie has had to master the art of life and leadership in order to maintain a presence in the industry and also fulfill the demands of her role at home. She shares some key ingredients to balancing life and work.

With Natalie's guidance, we will first discuss signs that your life and leadership might be out of balance. Second, we'll discuss the practical ingredients that are necessary to maneuver through a demanding career while fulfilling personal commitments at home.

## SIGNS YOU MIGHT BE OUT OF BALANCE

Here are some clues that your life might need some extra balancing. If any of these elements are present in your life, take extra precautions and see if you need to readjust.

### You Don't Have Supportive Family and Friends

One of the keys to a successful work-life balance is a supportive family. Natalie says that it would be impossible to be in a position of top leadership without the encouragement of her husband and children. When she got married, she never dreamed that her spouse would be so understanding of her schedule.[9] But she explains that he has been one of the most supportive husbands anyone could imagine. He is patient with her when she comes home late or when she doesn't come home very often. Natalie says she couldn't do it without his help.

"With my job, there is no 9–5," she explains. Natalie has to stay at work until the last customer leaves, even if that's four hours after closing time. Natalie's family realizes that she has to cater to the customers' needs. Natalie's children are understanding about their mom's schedule, knowing that her career path is very demanding.

Natalie's friends are also very supportive and respectful of the boundaries she places on her time. "Time is the single most precious thing for me," Natalie says. "I'm very limited with time. I do not have weekends. My weekends are during the week. If we vacation, I have to go with the schedule. If we choose to socialize, my friends have to socialize with my schedule."

Natalie asks her friends to schedule their dates with her, just like any customer or client would have to set an appointment. If they want to go to dinner, they will ask her, "This month, what days are you off?" The same goes for family. If they want to see her, they have to work around her schedule, which isn't always the same. Like school and district leaders, Natalie doesn't have a set schedule, and it changes often. Even if her schedule says she's working until six, it doesn't necessarily mean she'll be home at seven. Nevertheless, Natalie's support system has learned to be flexible.

Natalie is often too busy to attend social events, so she misses these things. Not wanting to go to these celebrations alone, her husband misses them too. Her family is willing to make this sacrifice. The sacrifice trickles down: the leader's sacrifice becomes their family's sacrifice. In order for a top leader's life to be in balance, the family and friends must be a team. They have to be in tune with the leader's priorities. They all have to work together to achieve the fruits of life.

"I rely on my family for a lot of things," Natalie says. "Having a strong support system at home enables me to be there and be present and have a successful career." On the other hand, she warns, "If you don't have an understanding family, it's not going to work, regardless of what industry you're in. Staying late, traveling for business several times a week—none of this will work out if you don't have a supportive family."

If your family is supportive and your spouse and children are fully behind you and their needs are being met, it's a sign your life is in balance. On the other hand, an unsupportive or resentful family is a sign that adjustments may need to be made. Maybe you need to add in some extra "lift," adding some additional supportive mentors and peer leaders who can help you carry the load of your family's negativity.

Perhaps you need to communicate more with your family about your priorities, dreams, and goals and listen to their priorities, dreams, and goals. Perhaps you need to consider spending more time with the people who are most important to you so they don't feel shortchanged. In any case, resentful family members may be a sign that something needs to be adjusted.

"Remember that you chose this path and a career, and you also chose to have a family," Natalie said. "You have to devote yourself to both. You have to juggle your work family and your home family. You have to find a way."

## You Resent Sacrifice

Another sign that your life and leadership balance is out of balance is when you yourself are starting to resent the sacrifices you are making. As a leader, your career is not easy. There are times when you must give up your desires in favor of the people you are leading. You make personal sacrifices for your time-intensive career. At times, you miss out on parties or events because you are working. If you find yourself resenting the sacrifice, it might be time to examine what you are prioritzing.

One personal sacrifice Natalie made is in the area of vacations. Before she became a top leader, she used to combine her vacation weeks and go on three-week vacations. But now, she's tied to the industry. She can't just disappear from the automotive business for weeks on end. She can only take off five or six days at a time, and she has to pick closer destinations. This is one of the personal sacrifices Natalie has made for her career.

Another sacrifice that many top-level female executives would not dream of making is in the beauty department. "I've learned to become a hairdresser and manicurist to save time," she says. "At a salon, you have to be there for three hours to get your hair done. I choose to do things at home so I can stay home and be there with the family to save the twenty minutes of driving."

Natalie also has to be picky about how she socializes. In her culture, there is always a christening, an event, or a wedding going on. But she can't go to all of them. She chooses the most important wedding to attend and misses the rest.

Like Natalie, you have likely experienced significant sacrifices in your career. On the other hand, if you are beginning to resent the sacrifices of top leadership, there may be something that needs to be adjusted. Maybe you need a break to get your priorities straight. Maybe you need to reexamine your commitment to your position or remind yourself of your why.

**You Lost Your Motivation**

Leadership comes in phases. Motivation ebbs and flows. There are times when the projects or challenges in front of you ignite the fire in your soul. You wake up in the morning knowing that you're in a position that you absolutely love. Everything seems super interesting and engaging. You get out of bed excited to find solutions and to find a way to get through the current challenge. You're as pumped about going to work as you would be if you were going on a fun trip.

For example, the pandemic was very fascinating and motivating for some leaders. Nothing was boring. Everything was new. Things were crazy, but it was an exciting, new challenge. Facing the controversy, competing agendas, and the groups aiming fire at you was stressful but fulfilling. Every day was different.

But sometimes, after the rush, there are times of discouragement and low motivation. There are lulls when you're not as excited about your job. You feel tired and stressed. Motivation is lacking. During these times, it's really critical to get in touch with what is wrong. Ask yourself, "What do I need right now?" It takes a lot of reflection to figure out what is lacking in your life.

If you are feeling super unmotivated, reflect and ask yourself, "What do I need right now to really caffeinate the soul and mind so I get out of this lull?" You have to ask yourself those types of questions. Otherwise, it becomes really easy to become so overwhelmed and unmotivated and say, "OK, this job's not for me." Remember that every position goes through phases. Don't jump straight to the idea of moving on to something else. Job-hopping won't solve those deeper problems.

If you're lacking motivation, ask yourself what you need. Maybe you just need rest. You need to take some time to relax and recharge. You need to change the work-life balance so that you have more time to spend with family or on self-care. When you take some time away, you'll be reenergized to continue your life of leadership.

On the other hand, maybe you need to shift the balance in the opposite direction. Maybe you need to create something new and exciting in your career to keep yourself occupied. You're the type of person who cannot stand being bored, and since you don't have a current challenge in front of you, you need to make one up. You need to create more work for yourself in the career arena so that your motivation rebounds.

For example, perhaps the schools in your district are moving forward and doing great. Everything is settled and at rest. You've had plenty of time to recharge. You're bored, and your motivation is waning. Maybe it's time to shake things up by dreaming up a new initiative to create motivation: "Let's start a universal preschool program!" "Let's implement restorative practices!" "Let's start a new community partnership program!"

When you start working on something that excites you, you notice that you once again have that motivation to get up in the morning. Low motivation may be a sign that you need to find a new task to keep you excited. In this case, you redistribute the weight by shifting the balance toward something more time-intensive at your job.

## HOW TO RESTORE BALANCE

Now that we've examined some signs that your life might be out of balance, let's look at a few practical ways you can restore the balance.

### Delegate and Collaborate

When you are overwhelmed, you may need to make modifications that honestly address your ever-changing workload capacity. During times of high stress, delegation can be an excellent solution. Ask yourself, "Which subordinate could I trust to help me carry out the tasks that are overwhelming me?"

As the weight of your career increases drastically, you must quickly integrate a balance adjustment. You can make a phone call to a colleague and say, "I really need your help with this difficult parent." You can tell a subordinate, "I could use some assistance with pulling data for the board report." You can ask an employee, "It would be very helpful for you to finish the last section of the compliance plan."

Collaboration is very important. Who could help you with the problem that is facing you? Who could brainstorm with you, giving you ideas about how to redistribute responsibilities and "weight" in the company?

Again, the goal is to not achieve a 50/50 balance at all times. But there are times when a slight modification can make a world of difference. These may not totally relieve all career stressors. But they do make a world of difference. They redistribute the weight of your leadership to a more manageable level.

## Unplug

When you're on vacation, it's important to scale back on your constant contact with your work world. Working hard is important, but so is playing hard while you're on break. When you do have time off, prioritize being really present with your people. You owe it to yourself to be able to breathe and not be bombarded with the pressures of work. Work could consume you tenfold during your time off if you let it. So set strict boundaries about which work tasks you will engage with during your time off.

How do you master this art? What tricks can help you set boundaries or strategize during your time off so you are not distracted? It's a constant struggle. Whereas sometimes entry-level employees can take weekends off with no distractions, the more promotions you obtain, the less you are truly off. There are always distractions, even on your day off. As a principal or superintendent, your evenings and weekends are consumed with events and athletics, in addition to the regular weekday commitments.

This is even more true for Natalie, as the automotive industry does not close on Saturdays and Sundays. Even when she's off, the business is still running. There are no weekends when everyone is off work. Someone is always working, even when she's relaxing. And they often call on her for answers and support, even when she's supposed to be resting.

Natalie has a strategy to deal with this. She makes a call or sends a text in the morning to make sure everything's going well. Throughout the day, she puts in two or three phone calls or texts to communicate with the team that's on the clock. She asks if everything is going well and if they need anything. She assures them they can reach her in case of emergency.

Aside from those check-ins, Natalie tries to be present with her family. If she wants uninterrupted time with loved ones, she lets her team know she's not going to be available for a while. "Hey, I'm going to dinner. I'm not going to be available for the next two or three hours." The key is communication.

Another strategy Natalie uses is making sure her team is well-trained so they can handle the pressures of work without her constant intervention. "My partners are well-prepared," Natalie says. "I have worked with them for many years. I feel safe leaving everything in their capable hands." As a result, they don't need to bother her on her days off because they can handle the challenges that arise. They take care of the problems on their own.

Natalie has also made intentional choices that allow her to truly unplug. "Some top-level positions will run you ragged," she says. "You will constantly be bothered and contacted, even when you're off." This is what happened when Natalie was the general sales manager for the business. She was constantly working, even on her days off. She was always in touch, in tune, making sure people were doing what they were supposed to do.

So Natalie chose to take a position that was one step lower. She readjusted the balance in her life so she could live a life that was more intentional and less pressured. She is now a member of a team of high-executive managers who work very well together. When she goes on vacation, she doesn't initiate any texts or calls. She waits to see how long she can go.

"It's been wonderful," she says.

> I can take an extended vacation, and they do not call me. They do not have hiccups. No one is nervous. And I have a great time off. Everyone has the training and the capability to handle the situations that come up, and they do what they do. The team respects how important it is for me to have a long, relaxing time with my family.

When necessary, you may need to make career adjustments in order to give you more time to rest and recharge.

## Embrace Challenge

When your life is off balance, you may need to adjust your circumstances, as we saw in the last few sections. But other times, you may simply need to adjust your mindset. For Natalie, letting go of perfectionism has been a big part of her new mindset. In the beginning of her career, she was very stressed about juggling the work-life balance. She wanted to be the perfect wife, the perfect mom, and the perfect employee. In a male-dominated industry, she was working twice as hard just to show her cohorts that she knew just as much. She could feel the anxiety and the pressure.

But as time went on, she began to see work-life balance through a different lens. She let go of perfectionism. And she stopped using the word "stressed." She grimaces every time people do a simple chore and say, "I'm so stressed out." She believes this word contributes to the mindset that we can't handle life. Instead, Natalie adjusts her thinking.

"It's a mindset," she says. She doesn't let the idea of stress consume her. Thinking about stress only makes the problem worse. "I like stress," Natalie says. "For me, stress is life. Stress is work. Stress is living. I don't think of it as stress." She recognizes that almost any problem that comes her way can be fixed. Even if the problem can't be fixed at the moment, she knows that with help, time, and a different viewpoint, anything can be fixed. There's no reason to feel stressed.

So if your life is out of balance, maybe you just need to see things differently. Maybe you can shift the balance by shifting your mindset. Realize that stress and a certain amount of pain are normal, healthy parts of growing. Problems that are weighing on you and getting you out of balance might not be as bad as you think if you just shift your mindset.

## Recover the Love

Natalie shares that another key to coping with work-life balance is to love what you do. After twenty years in the industry, she still says without hesitation, "I love what I do." She encourages other leaders: "You have to love your job. If you don't love what you do, it just becomes misery." Even challenges and stress become tolerable if you are truly passionate about your career. If your life is out of balance, see if you can recover some of the enthusiasm, joy, and love that you had when you first started your career. If not, it may be time to make a change.

## Practice Self-Care

As you delegate tasks to others, cut down on your workload, adjust your thinking, and unplug, you are free to truly take care of yourself. Focus on your self-care. After all, a leader is only able to serve others well when they serve themselves well.

As a leader, you will constantly have to survive tough situations and battle stress. Every time you turn around, there's a new problem you have to conquer. It's important to take time for rest so that you can build the resilience you need to overcome every obstacle.

You need to take care of yourself so you can keep up your long-term momentum. You must remember that you're in a marathon, not a sprint. And this includes taking care of yourself and maintaining a good work-life balance.

Why is it important to stay balanced? It's all about building sustainable leadership that can pass the test of time. Without balance, you will constantly lose yourself in the day-to-day grind. But when you refuel yourself regularly, your resilience will last a lifetime.

## AIR TRAFFIC CONTROL

During a preflight checklist, an aircraft needs to make sure its weight and balance are correctly distributed. In the same way, you need to prepare yourself for the next adventure by making sure your work and life are balanced. Make sure your values are clear so that you can maintain a wise balance in the midst of changing circumstances.

- Pay attention to things that are out of whack, such as resentment in yourself or your family.
- Reset your mindset. Your job is not a chore if you love what you do, even the stressful parts.
- Delegation, collaboration, and self-care are critical approaches to redistributing life leadership balance.
- Communicate with your friends and family and make sure they're fully on board with your career plans.
- Embrace sacrifice. Life is not easy, and leadership is not a walk in the park. Understand and embrace this reality.
- Unplug. Take time to recharge, completely free from the distractions of work.
- Long-lasting leadership. Remember the reason you rest: so you can build a sustainable impact.
- Make sure these elements are in place before you take flight. If not, ask yourself how you can strengthen the areas that are lacking.

## NOTES

1. Morgan Lee, "20 Cuban Pastors and Spouses Killed in Plane Crash," *Christianity Today*, last modified May 21, 2018. Accessed November 30, 2022, https://www.christianitytoday.com/news/2018/may/cuba-pastors-spouses-killed-in-havana-plane-crash-nazarene.html.

2. Ahona Sengupta, "'Weight and Balance' Errors Caused Deadly Cuba Air Crash That Killed 112 People," last modified May 17, 2019. Accessed November 30, 2022, https://www.news18.com/news/world/weight-and-balance-errors-caused-deadly-cuba-air-crash-that-killed-112-people-2144243.html.

3. "NTSB: Improper Loading Caused Challenger Jet Crash," *Aviation Software Solutions*. Accessed November 30, 2022, https://www.eflite.com/news/aircraft_weight_balance_crash_1.php.

4. FAA, *Weight and Balance Handbook* (Newcastle, WA: Aviation Supplies & Academics, Inc., 2016), 15. Accessed on US Department of Transportation, November 30, 2021, https://www.faa.gov/regulations_policies/handbooks_manuals/aviation/media/faa-h-8083-1.pdf.

5. Mary F. Silitch, "Out-of-limit cg Might Have Led to TEB Crash," *AINonline*, last modified October 31, 2006. Accessed February 13, 2023, https://www.ainonline

.com/aviation-news/aviation-international-news/2006-10-31/out-limit-cg-might-have-led-teb-crash.

6. "NTSB: Improper Loading."
7. "NTSB: Improper Loading."
8. FAA, *Weight and Balance*.
9. Business executive, in conversation with the author, September 1, 2022. Name changed for privacy.

*Chapter 3*

# Security Screening for Hijackers

## *Avoiding Time Mismanagement and Micromanaging*

Hijackers. They freak us out. The mere thought of a plane being hijacked is enough to make anyone break out in a sweat. The question on every traveler's mind is, "What would I do if I was on that plane?"

On September 11, 2001, horror stories played on every television screen around the country. Those same stories replayed dozens of times in our minds and imaginations. Even today, we relive these scenes every September, reminded of the tragic results of hijackings. We recall the passengers' cell phone recordings that described the terror of being on the plane while the hijackers were attempting to take down the aircraft. We are inspired by the bravery of those who attempted to defeat the hijackers.

Though it was impressed by the courage of those who fought the hijackers, the government recognized that the most effective way to prevent hijackings was to thwart hijackers before the plane took flight. After 2001, security in airports has increased exponentially. Terrified by the thought of hijackers lurking in every seat, airport officials are determined to weed out potential aggressors before they ever get on a plane. As a result, every traveler now has to go through a strict security inspection.

Belts, bags, and coats have to be removed and carefully examined. Pockets are emptied. Shoes are taken off. Laptops and devices are placed on a conveyor belt. Then, as journalist David Schaper commented, we "step into high-resolution, full-body scanners, while our bags go through 3D-imaging X-ray machines. And don't forget to take your liquids of 3.4 ounces or less out of your carry-on."[1] Anything that resembles a weapon, "like the box-cutters used by the 9/11 hijackers," is prohibited.[2]

Before 2001, friends and families could accompany their loved ones right up to the gate. But after 2001, only the passengers themselves are allowed near the airplane gate. Air travelers are accustomed to long security lines.

They begin arriving at airports earlier to allow for sufficient time to board the plane. No longer can curious kids visit the cockpit; new security regulations "required that . . . cockpit doors be reinforced, and more federal air marshals be put on flights."[3]

The security measures were effective. Before 2001, there were an average of twenty to sixty global hijackings per year.[4] After 2001, there has been a drastic decline. In 2021, there were only three hijackings globally.[5]

So how does this apply to top leadership? Just like hijackers sometimes sneak onto planes, dangerous and career-deadly tendencies can sneak into your leadership style. There are two types of dangerous hijackers that can sneak into your organization: time management problems and micromanagement problems.

## TIME MANAGEMENT

The first hijacker that can disrupt your smooth flight is an urgent but unnecessary task. When you least realize it, these can take over your day. You set out toward a particular goal in leadership, but dozens of tiny things begin to hijack your time. They sneak in unnoticed, disguised as crucial, important objectives.

Leaders often are in a whirlwind of chaos, constantly putting out fires. Their life is full of stressors, and they take the hits at every turn. Urgent tasks seem to grab the leader, beat them up, and leave them on the sidelines, while these impetuous hijackers take control and direct the leader's day toward their own objectives.

How can we keep urgent tasks from hijacking our lives? Yolanda Valdez shares some excellent thoughts pertaining to time management. With nine years of experience as a superintendent, as well as many years of experience as an instructional assistant, classroom teacher, and assistant superintendent, she has much to say about the hijackers of time management. She has also spent time as a high school principal, arguably one of the most time-intensive principalships that exist. She has a wealth of lessons she can share about time management in leadership.

### Become Self-Aware

Yolanda says the first step in time management is introspection. As you try to improve your time-management skills, your first look needs to be inward. You need to examine how you lead, how you manage, and how you supervise.[6] Before you begin to try to address the issue of how to prioritize between important issues and urgent issues, you must know what your own natural tendencies are. Your first focus needs to be on you.

You will naturally go in the way that is easiest for you, so you need to become self-aware about your habits and the ways you tend to waste time. Where are your inborn natural tendencies? What are your natural priorities? You need to deeply understand your own habits and propensities so you can make the extra effort to overcome those tendencies.

For example, some people are naturally methodical. They waste time by going too slowly and focusing on perfection. This person needs to look within, realize their natural tendencies, and work on feeling a sense of urgency within their job.

On the other hand, some people are too action-based. They are so focused on putting out fires and solving urgent problems that they lose sight of the long-term values and big picture. That is how Yolanda would describe herself.

"I'm enthusiastic and I want to get things done yesterday," she says. "I know that about myself. I have to work really hard to slow down, to become more conscious and steady." She says that every day, she intentionally focuses on pacing herself. It's the only way she can overcome her out-of-balance emphasis on action, enthusiasm, and results.

Yolanda recommends personality tests like DISC training. These are so important because they force you to look inside, which is a critical step to take before you can start executing your goals.

## Focus on Getting Healthy

Yolanda says the next step toward time management is to prioritize your own physical, emotional, and mental health. Before you even talk about organization skills, you need to focus on yourself first. That has to come into place before anything else. If that's not intact, the work can't be done.

We must be very well centered on ourselves, our priorities, and our goals to gift ourselves time to take care of the number one priority: health. We need to take time to actually sleep. How many times are you working in the middle of the night and don't have time to sleep? Or how many times are you thinking and worrying all night? There's a great cure for that. It's called a non-habit-forming nighttime sleeping aid. When push comes to shove, this tool can help you get some shut-eye so you can be refreshed to solve the problems in the morning.

## Reflect on Your Goals and Values

Third, carve out reflection time. If we, as leaders, are not reflective, we're going to continue making the same mistakes and missteps. We'll fail to move the organization forward. During your personal reflection time, you'll spend time creating that personal leadership agenda that you will be spending 40–50 percent of your time on. You'll ask yourself, "What are the big boulders? And how are we moving them forward?"

As the CEO, superintendent, or leader of a big organization, you have a great responsibility to follow your organization's agenda. Your board will constantly dictate to you, "These are urgent matters you have to attend to, and if you don't attend to them, they will become huge." But in addition to your organizational agenda, you must also develop and follow your own personal agenda. You must take time to ask yourself, "Where am I taking my organization? Am I walking my talk? Where is my time being spent?"

Yolanda shares that her "big boulders" are making sure her students are ready for college, career, and community so they can compete in a global economy. During her times of reflection, she asks herself, "How are we doing that? What is happening in the classroom that is moving that forward? What am I doing as an instructional leader of this district? Am I spending time on the important stuff?"

Many times, we think we're focusing on our big goals. But in reality, our calendar doesn't reflect that. We may say we're instructional leaders. But what is our everyday agenda? Are we really moving our instructional practices forward? Does it show up on our calendars?

It's vitally important to know ourselves thoroughly, understand ourselves deeply, and work with ourselves to achieve our goals. Otherwise, we will be carried away with the urgent needs of the organization. We must ensure that our time is managed in such a way that we can focus on the most critical work.

## Put Your Values on the Calendar

For a superintendent or top leader, time is very, very scarce. Time is the resource that is in the shortest supply, so you have to schedule time for important things. Calendar them into your life.

Do you want to pop in and visit your classified staff during their professional learning? Calendar it in. Do you tend to procrastinate on mid-year reviews? Schedule a specific time to work on it. If you don't calendar those really important tasks that move the district's vision and goals forward, they won't happen. To accomplish your important goals, you have to schedule them very consciously.

If you schedule weekly cabinet meetings with your core team of associates, you'll be less likely to allow other things to interrupt this commitment. Make this a sacred time on your calendar. You may miss one occasionally, but in general, these things happen because they're scheduled. That's the key.

During your time of reflection, you will determine what is important. Now you need to actually put it on your calendar.

## Plan a Daily Schedule that Reflects Your Goals

Every day, Yolanda's schedule reflects what is important to her. She gets up in the morning and spends some time exercising and reflecting. During winter, she gets on her elliptical. During good weather, she's out walking the acres of her property in the country. As she's doing that, she's utilizing this time to ponder her vision and goals. She either problem-solves an issue at work through listening to TED Talks and YouTube videos, or she reflects on something that needs her attention in order move forward. She starts her day with downtime.

By the time she jumps into the shower, she's finished with the YouTube video or whatever she's listening to. While she puts on her makeup, she starts making phone calls. It's a perfect time to talk. People are driving in to work between seven and eight, so she can talk with her directors while they drive. She asks questions about things that happened or concerns she saw at schools during her visits. The directors are always so busy, so she takes advantage of their morning commute to address items that need to get done in order to move the important goals forward.

After that, she makes visits to schools. About 80 percent of the time, she visits one of the schools in the district before she even walks into her office. She knows that when she walks into her office, she will be bombarded with a list of urgent things to attend to.

This is why Yolanda visits schools before she even has a chance to find out what's going wrong in the office. She wants to make sure that she's attending to the important things, not just the urgent things. She chooses to prioritize the things that align with her agenda for her organization and students, rather than solely tending to urgent matters that don't contribute to the progress she wants to make.

Yolanda alternates every day, seeing a minimum of three schools a week. Many times, if a school is having some issues or the principal is really new, she sees them more often. When she arrives at a school, she starts with positivity.

"Who are the teachers that you're really proud of?" she asks the principals. "Let's walk into those classrooms." After she establishes a positive baseline, she then addresses concerns. "Who are the teachers that you're working with? Where's your concern?"

After brainstorming solutions to the problems, she then checks in with the principals to ensure they're still on the same page with her values and goals. "Are we aligned in expectations?" she asks. Yolanda agrees with Simon Sinek: everything we think, act, and communicate needs to be centered on our why. So she communicates clearly with principals about how they are moving the district's important work forward.

After school visits, Yolanda finally heads to the office. But does she sit down and read all her emails? No, absolutely not. "Emails are poisonous," Yolanda says. "You've been copied on three hundred emails a day. You could sit there and answer emails all day."

Instead, Yolanda spends her day meeting with people, moving the district's initiatives forward. She sits in on meetings. She goes to data chats. She tries to attend all instructional rounds, or at least the debrief. She participates in studies so she can help people understand and see how important that work is. Her priority is time that is face-to-face with people. She knows that human interaction is what moves the important work forward.

In the evening, she joins the community by attending sporting events and parent education sessions. She comes home, has a few hours to herself, and ends her day with emails. If she's very tired, she scans her emails and replies only to the urgent ones or very important ones that are going to move things forward. Other days, she goes through all the emails, which can take a couple of hours.

Yolanda's day clearly reflects her goals and values. Your day may look a little different if you're in charge of a larger district. In fact, you may be saying, "I could never swing a schedule like that. There's no way that a superintendent of 40,000 students would ever have the time to prioritize being at school sites." However, the same principles apply to you, even if they are implemented differently. Instead of visiting the schools yourself, you may delegate that work to your directors, who report directly to you and support you. For you, the important work becomes face-to-face time with the directors so they can prioritize face-to-face time with the schools.

## Actively Prioritize the Important

As a leader, you're always going to have those urgent calls. Constantly. You can be out and about, visiting a school, focusing on something important, and you suddenly get a call from HR or the MOT: "Yeah, we really need you to come see this."

What do you do then? You say, "I am busy doing something important that moves the district's goals forward. Make the decision. I trust you. And then I will come see you, and I'll talk to you after I am done with what I am doing."

Yolanda says that there are times when she leaves what she's doing and attends to something back at the office. But in general, she makes it a priority to stay present with whatever important thing she has set out to do.

This isn't easy for Yolanda, and it may not be easy for you, either. Like Yolanda, your natural urge may be to go extinguish that urgent fire ASAP. But if you have looked inside yourself and consciously worked on yourself, you can stay focused on the important things. Even if it's difficult, you need to be very calculated in sending the message, "These are the big boulders and they're so big that I choose be present."

## Trust Your Leaders

What is one reason we let urgent matters hijack our days? We don't always entrust staff to take care of what they are highly capable of handling on their own. In order to manage your time effectively, you must trust your subordinates to handle the urgent stuff. You can tell your leaders, "You take care of that, and I'll circle back later and come see how that went." When they handle emergencies for you, it frees you to stay focused on the important things in your life and business.

But if you choose to micromanage your staff, even when they're well trained and prepared to handle it on their own, it's a recipe for disaster. Not only do you allow urgent matters to hijack your time because you don't trust anyone else to do them for you, but you also become the hijacker of your staff members' lives.

## MICROMANAGING

The second hijacker that is trying to sneak into your life is the hijacker of micromanaging. Without knowing it, you unconsciously hijack the creativity of your staff. Full of good intentions and wanting high-quality results that only you can produce, you try to control your subordinates' every move. Sound familiar?

Why is it so easy to want to be in control? Because you feel confident that you can do the job better than anyone else can. After all, how did you get to this position that you're in? You got here by doing the work, doing it intensely, and doing it in a very calculated way. You developed a certain amount of pride thinking that no one could do the work like you could. And to a degree, that's true. No matter how humble the leader, every top leader has a little bit of that arrogance, because it's true that you ascended to that position through your own hard work.

That's why deferring to your staff's style, ideas, and approaches doesn't come naturally. When you choose to let go of something that helped get you to where you are today, it's not easy. However, it's important to counteract your natural hard-working, micromanaging tendencies and allow others to take control. If not, we hijack our staff's lives.

Look at it from a teacher's perspective. When you started out as a classroom teacher or lower-level administrator, you had creative ideas about solving problems, approaching issues, and teaching and guiding your students. You didn't want a top leader to micromanage you, take control of your life, and make decisions for you. In the same way, you need to let your subordinates exercise their creative gifts. When a leader doesn't trust their staff and isn't involving them in important decisions, he or she is basically hijacking or hacking their staff's power.

How can you avoid being a hijacker on your own airplane of leadership? Each of us needs to learn how to implement better "airport security" so that our own controlling tendencies never get aboard the plane of leadership. What do those security measures look like?

## Equip Your Leaders

The most significant way to avoid micromanaging others is to make sure your subordinates are equipped to lead on their own. The more you train them, the more you trust them. And the more you trust them, the more confident you are about turning them loose to solve urgent problems without you.

District superintendent Anne talks about how she trains her leaders. She spends a lot of time with her assistant superintendents, talking about philosophy, direction, ethics, and decision-making. She wants them to be thoroughly aware of the ways she makes decisions.[7] Anne's leaders always know where she stands on every issue. If a situation came up where they needed to defer to Anne's authority, they would automatically ask and answer the question "What would Anne do?" They can then make decisions that are based on Anne's philosophy and ethos, which are in turn consistent with board direction, board goals, and what's in the best interest of the district.

Anne wants the leaders under her to make decisions in the vein of her philosophy because she knows her philosophy fits with the board. That's the funnel. Anne's job is to find out what the board wants and how they want things done. Then her cabinet's job is to make decisions that are in the best interest of Anne, the board, and the community. The number one way to avoid micromanagement is to make sure you spend a lot of time talking about belief systems and goals so that everyone is very clear on the district's goals, the strategic mission of the board of education, and the district's values.

As you train your staff in the mission, values, and decision-making process of your district, it's important to be clear that you're not expecting people to just fall in line and agree. Anne doesn't force her staff to become carbon copies of her. She encourages her subordinates to be in touch with their own thoughts, opinions, and knowledge on a subject.

At the same time, subordinate leaders must understand the importance of their superior's values and how their decisions are made. Like an hourglass, decisions can be made in either direction, but they all must be consistent in values so that you can be successful as a superintendent, district, and community. That's critically important.

If you know you've hired well and that your subordinates have the training, skillset, and guidance they need, then you don't need to micromanage them. If your leaders know the expectations, you can trust them to lead on their own. If you've clearly passed on your vision and goals so that your staff members understand where your district is going, you can be confident they will handle situations in a way that would align with you.

## Talk about Specific Situations

In addition to passing on general mission, philosophy, and values, it's important to spend a lot of time talking through specific situations as they come up. Spend a lot of time with your subordinates upfront, training them about how to approach specific situations. For example, the first year Anne is with a new cabinet member, she spends a lot of time with them in extended cabinet meetings. Rather than holding individual meetings with the new staff members, she invites them to longer group cabinet meetings where they can observe her seasoned leaders' decision-making processes in action.

During these long cabinet meetings, the new members can hear the consistent philosophy and thinking process around all decisions. Every member of her cabinet needs to see how the others make decisions. The curriculum person needs to listen to the HR person, who needs to listen to the businessperson, who needs to listen to the equity person, and who needs to listen to the communication person. Each of them needs to see that there's consistency in how decisions are made. Through group meetings, everyone is privy to the thought process and the discussion.

As much as you can, try to ensure that leaders aren't making decisions over other people's areas. Make decisions together, and allow everyone to observe how decisions are made in their department and other departments.

Once you're confident that your subordinate leaders understand your mission, vision, values, and decision-making process, you can set them free to make their own decisions. You no longer have to micromanage. You can trust them to take care of urgent situations without your direct oversight. When situations come up that they can't handle on their own, they can take them to you.

## Empower Your Leaders

Sometimes, leaders need a friendly push to encourage them to make decisions on their own. You must empower them to act on their own and not depend on you for every little thing. You must actively show them that you trust them.

In Anne's large district of over sixteen thousand students, there are multiple departments, including human resources, business, education services, communication, diversity, equity, and inclusion. All decisions flow through assistant superintendents or directors. They all have hundreds of things they're responsible for every day. On any given day, Anne spends a lot of time helping these leaders decide what's a cabinet-level decision and what's not. She doesn't want everything coming to the cabinet—who has time for that? She spends a lot of time talking about what are big, important components and what are smaller decisions that can be made independently.

When a cabinet member puts an item on the cabinet agenda and Anne realizes it's something so small that it doesn't need to be talked about in the cabinet, she empowers them to make their own decisions. She tells them, "You've got to make that decision yourself and take responsibility for that. You know our values, goals, and ethics, so make the decision within those parameters. You've got to make those decisions on your own."

Instead of micromanaging, it's better to give your employees an end goal and let them accomplish it however they wish. Be very clear:

> This is what I need the end to look like. How you get there is up to you. There are countless decisions to make between the decision and the outcome. And those decisions are yours. Whatever process you use, I need it to end up like this.

You have to empower your leaders to do that.

For example, when the curriculum department is tasked with textbook adoption, Anne does not necessarily involve herself in the ins and outs of the process of curriculum adoption. She trusts that the curriculum director will absolutely meet the end goal of board adoption of new or updated curriculum often required by state legislation.

Sure, Anne will have check-ins to understand where the process is along the way and how it is progressing. This way, she is also available to be a thought partner with her director if need be. However, she will absolutely not interfere with the process or unnecessarily insert herself into making these decisions. She knows that micromanaging the curriculum director would only compromise the integrity of the curriculum adoption process itself.

Make a point to teach your directors not to micromanage their subordinates. Anne teaches her assistant superintendents to work with their directors the same way she works with them. "What are you empowering your directors to do?" she asks her assistant superintendents. "I don't want to be involved in making decisions at the assistant superintendent level, so you have to empower your directors to do that."

What do you do if you have a subordinate who is a chronic micromanager? It's not necessarily your job to fix your staff members—if that were even possible. Instead, it's your job to bring your subordinate's awareness to their leadership style. Help them realize that micromanaging is not a good use of their time. Be very clear and honest with this staff member. Tell them, "You need to allow your people to make those decisions and run those projects."

## Should We Micromanage Millennials?

Perhaps you feel a special temptation to micromanage millennials. "They just aren't like Gen Xers," you may say, shaking your head. "That's why I need to constantly be on their case, micromanaging them, to make sure they get something done." The same thing could be said of Gen Z and the following generations. The generational gap may tempt you to seize control. You've heard rumors about these young people's bad work habits, and you feel you have to take care of those problems before they happen.

In some ways, the younger generations may need some extra coaching. But that doesn't mean we need to micromanage them. Instead, we need to mentor them into being stronger leaders. If someone has generational blind spots, your job as a leader is to coach them up.

If you are concerned that millennials need extra micromanaging, try to remember this important fact: Yes, they may fail. And if they fail, then they fail. There has to be some failure in order to learn and grow. Remember that you, as a leader, have failed. We've all failed. But after we fail once, we learn from it. It hurts pretty bad, and we learn what not to do in the future. The same is true of your millennial worker. Failure is not always a bad thing.

Because millennials and Gen Zers may have different work styles than you, there may be automatic assumptions about how they are going to do certain things. True, there may be reasons why these stereotypes exist. Perhaps these younger generations have new, creative ideas that the older generations can learn from.

If you are very concerned about millennials or Gen Zers failing, you can implement stopgap measures and check-in situations. But if you micromanage them, you're forever going to be holding them up. They're going to always want your opinion, and they'll never be able to function on their own. Instead, you need to empower them and allow them to grow.

## AIR TRAFFIC CONTROL

The thought of what it actually feels like to have a hijacker strip the pilot and passengers of control is nothing short of terrifying. And no staff member wants you as a leader to hijack their creative process, their leadership ability, or their ability to grow.

- Just like passengers trust the airline industry and the pilot, you must trust your staff to arrive at the destination safely—even if they don't take the same route you would.
- When you trust your leaders to take care of urgent matters, it frees you up to pursue the important parts of leadership.
- Don't let urgent tasks hijack the deeper visions, goals, and mission of your district.

## NOTES

1. David Schaper, "It Was Shoes On, No Boarding Pass Or ID. But Airport Security Forever Changed On 9/11," September 10, 2021. Accessed December 16, 2022, https://www.npr.org/2021/09/10/1035131619/911-travel-timeline-tsa.

2. Schaper, "It Was Shoes On."

3. David Koenig, "How 9/11 Changed Air Travel: More Security, Less Privacy," September 6, 2021. Accessed September 28, 2023, https://apnews.com/article/how-sept-11-changed-flying-1ce4dc4282fb47a34c0b61ae09a024f4.

4. Hannah Ritchie, Joe Hassell, Edouard Mathieu, Cameron Appel, and Max Rose, "Terrorism," last modified October 2022. Accessed February 13, 2023, https://ourworldindata.org/terrorism#airline-hijackings.

5. "Number of Aircraft Hijackings in the Aviation Industry Worldwide from 1990 to 2021," *Statista*, last modified April 12, 2022. Accessed November 30, 2022, https://www.statista.com/statistics/1240246/aircraft-hijackings-worldwide/.

6. Yolanda Valdez (superintendent), in discussion with the author, January 5, 2023.

7. Superintendent #1, in discussion with the author, January 9, 2023. Name changed for privacy.

*Part 2*

# EN-ROUTE

*Chapter 4*

# Reading Your Instruments
## *Charisma, Clarity, and Communication*

As a plane lifts off the ground and circles higher into the sky, the landscape stretches below like a green and brown patchwork quilt. The sky is sunny above the aircraft. For a moment, the pilot wants to just kick back, close his eyes, and relax.

Yet even while the pilot is relaxing, it's important to stay vigilant. Even when things are going well, the pilot must constantly be in touch with what the control panel is telling them. The pilot's instruments give information about the airspeed, motor revolution speed, direction, the aircraft's longitudinal rotation, and meteorological conditions.[1] When pilots get so comfortable with their flight that they don't pay attention to the instruments, it will put the flight in jeopardy—like the F-35 plane that crashed in April 2019 because the pilot was not paying attention to what the airplane's instruments were indicating.[2]

Just like pilots read their instruments, leaders must read the attitudes and responses of the people they are communicating with. Otherwise, their leadership is headed for disaster. Just like pilots use an "Attitude Indicator" (yes, attitude, not altitude), a "Heading Indicator," and a "Turn Coordinator" to keep on track,[3] leaders must learn to sense the *attitudes* of the audience so they can decide which way to *head* and how to shift gears and *turn* when necessary. You'll need to read the room so you can lead the room.

Unlike a classroom teacher, whose audience can be limited to parents and kids, site and district leaders must communicate with a wide and diverse audience. They must learn to read the responses of elected officials, school board members, fellow administrators, counselors, community members, parents, teachers, and kids.

With such a diverse audience, it's important to learn to constantly read the emotions and needs of the people you are talking to, just like a pilot reads the control panels. Depending on which group of people you are working with, you will need to choose a varied and unique approach that suits the audience's needs. Leaders who are relatable and easily connect with even the most difficult of people are the ones who gain a great deal of respect.

When you're paying attention to reading the room, you know when to be tough on somebody, when to beat around the bush, when to be gentle, and how to poise something. Depending on the needs of your audience, you may choose to be vocal or to sit back and listen. Your listeners may need you to be more aggressive and direct, or they may need you to just sit there and nod.

There is an art to reading a room, knowing your audience's needs, and naturally interacting with each person. But how does that art develop? What are some of the practical skills that will help you read the feedback your audience is giving you?

## LEARN PEOPLE'S STORIES

Reading a room is easier when you are leaning in. Leaning in means demonstrating a true interest in others' stories, in others' experiences, and ultimately in wanting to see others succeed. Caring about others' stories makes life easier in the long run. Yes, it takes more time in the short term, but it is significantly more rewarding.

Terri Rufert, a leader who has served in administration for twenty-eight years, found this out the hard way. At first, she faced all employees and coworkers as problems to be solved. She made assumptions and tried to fix people and situations quickly. But after several tough experiences, Terri learned how to lean in and care about each individual's story.

Terri has always demonstrated a very honest, in-your-face persona. As a lead teacher, her blunt personality didn't always go over well. One day, a teacher needed someone to relieve her so she could go off duty at the appointed time. She asked Terri to help, but Terri was busy. Her students were eating in her classroom, and Terri had briefly stepped out to get some silverware. She needed to get back.[4]

"I have kids in my room waiting for me," Terri told the girl. "Call the office and they'll take care of it." Of course, at face value, this seemed to be a rational and reasonable response.

Terri hurried back to her room and thought nothing about it again until the day she received some not-so-pleasing news: the girl had filed a grievance against Terri. Terri was ticked, so she called the teacher out.

"What do you mean I didn't help you out?" Terri asked. "The superintendent and I both told you to call the office. But you didn't listen to me." Looking back, Terri can see that her perspective was all wrong. She was self-focused, and her tone of voice and facial expression were communicating, "I'm right. I don't care about you. You are ridiculous."

Thankfully, the grievance didn't go anywhere. Years later, the woman reached out to Terri again. "I just want to let you know that I'm better now," the teacher said.

Terri emailed her back and said, "What do you mean?"

The teacher replied, "I've been in therapy ever since you didn't help me when you were the lead teacher."

"Why would you go to therapy for that?" Terri asked.

"You never valued me. You never cared about me."

Those words literally destroyed Terri. She'd always thought of herself as a people person. "I love people. How could she say that?" Terri agonized. She had to do a lot of soul-searching and praying.

Eventually, Terri got the chance to hear this teacher's life story. This woman had been abused, and the abuse contributed to her perception of Terri. Learning the teacher's story was an important lesson for Terri. When that teacher asked for Terri's help many years ago, she asked for more than just lunch coverage. She wanted Terri's personal attention and care. And Terri realized that if she had taken the time to lean in and learn the woman's deeper needs, the entire interaction would have gone much better.

"Realize you don't know the other person's story," Terri advises. Then, take the time to get to know their story. "Listening to other people's stories is genuinely interesting. I start feeling for others with more empathy and compassion."

Now, when an angry person calls, Terri's first question is, "What is really bothering you? Help me understand what is really bothering you, because I'm not quite understanding, and I want to. I want this to be a win-win for everyone." The more she understands, the better she communicates.

Terri shares another example that shows the importance of digging deeper and finding out other people's stories so you can understand their fears and desires. A short time after the teacher incident, Terri transferred to another school district as an administrator. She was significantly younger than the other staff members, and her appearance and clothing style clearly demonstrated her age.

One day, one of the members of the union came to her and said, "Hey, if you want us to listen to you, you probably shouldn't dress the way you do. Your skirt should be a little longer."

Terri was obviously not happy. "What difference should that make?" she thought. But she kept her mouth shut, clamped her irritation inside, went home, and called her mother to let off some steam.

Her mom remained calm. "What do you think that lady is really saying to you, Terri?"

"What do you mean?"

Her mom continued to probe. "When you were a teacher, what made you such a good teacher?"

"The relationships I had with the kids. I got to know them and helped each kid be the best they could be."

"Can you get to know your staff just like you got to know your former students?"

"What do you mean, Mom?"

"Dig deeper. Find out what that lady was really saying with her snide comment. I bet there's more to it than the way you were dressing. My suggestion is you go back and talk to that person and ask what's going on."

"Mom, that's ridiculous."

Despite her frustration, Terri followed her mom's advice. Terri decided to get to know her staff and find out what made them tick. When she went back and talked to the woman, she found out about her staff's genuine fears.

Some of the employees struggled with Terri being in this new position. They were afraid she was going to change everything. They found it difficult to relate to her bubbly personality. Under the surface, their fears were valid.

The conversation was a major turning point for her. Terri began to work harder to learn other people's stories instead of assuming it was all about her. It wasn't always easy; some of Terri's staff had thick emotional walls and were even harder to relate to than resistant kids. But Terri kept trying, and eventually she succeeded. As she heard her staff members' stories, she learned to walk a mile in someone else's shoes.

## SELF-REFLECT

In addition to dealing with her staff's baggage, Terri had to deal with her own. One day, a staff member came up to Terri and said, "You just think you're going to change everything because you know everything."

Terri replied, "No I don't."

But she soon realized there was more to this situation than met the eye. "I wasn't digging deep enough," she says. When she started soul-searching, she found things that weren't pretty. She realized she often did think she knew a lot. Like many leaders, Terri was a problem-solver and fixer.

Teachers would come to her, and she would try to solve their problems. Since she was good at problem-solving, she thought she had all the answers. Confident and even egotistical, she was a taskmaster who could get things done. Like many leaders, Terri sometimes forgot the people behind the problems.

Terri had never realized that teachers don't always want their problems solved. They want to be cared for. She only focused on solving the problems in her career. Determined to change, Terri consulted trusted mentors and found answers in her faith. Terri learned to dig down to the roots of what was going on inside of her and inside her employees.

As she self-reflected further, Terri noticed that she often interrupted her subordinates in staff meetings when she could tell they weren't getting their point across. What was the reason for her impolite interruptions? At the time, she would have rationalized that she didn't want them to fail. She interrupted to add clarity and make sure their communication succeeded.

But now she realizes that her behavior stems from her own fear and insecurity. In the process, her "I know best" mentality was getting in the way of her staff members' growth.

Any time you get frustrated or angry at your staff or the decisions they make, take a moment to self-reflect. Brian Miller encourages you to engage in serious self evaluation: Are you mad because your pride has been hurt, or because a true wrong or injustice is being done? If it's just your pride that's been hurt, you can move past that and carry on. But if a wrong or injustice is genuinely happening, then you need to address it, confront it, and work to make it right. If it's just your pride, let it go. Swallow that and move forward.[5]

Terri, like most effective leaders, had to be willing to shift the focus away from herself and instead put the focus on others.

## DEVELOP CHARISMA

When it comes to charisma, you either have it or you don't. Have you ever been in the presence of someone who just seems to light up every room? Have you watched that person truly work the room? Their secret is charisma.

This type of leader doesn't just facilitate conversations and get tasks done. They have a noticeable, polished presence. They are sought-after and easily approachable. When this leader gives a presentation or facilitates a meeting, people are drawn to them and highly engaged with what they are saying.

Charisma is defined as "a type of leadership that combines charm, interpersonal connection, and persuasiveness to motivate others."[6] Charismatic leaders know their audiences well enough to "motivate and inspire their teams toward a greater goal . . . by creating a sense of trust, passion, and purpose."[7] As a leader, if you lack charisma, your ability to connect with people will greatly suffer. Chances are, it already has.

Now that we know what charisma is, let's also define what charisma is not. Charisma is not a slimy politician feeding the crowd a buffet of BS. We have all been in the unfortunate company of these leaders, who come across as fake. We see leaders who come off as manipulative and disingenuous. Their bedside manner appears to be nothing short of personal gain. Quite frankly, this type of attitude can be a major turnoff to those they are trying to lead.

These leaders subscribe to the "it's all about me" mentality. Chances are, you have a name in your mind right now, and images of that person make your stomach turn as you are reading this. As this leader talks, you want to say, "Just close your mouth now", while you are trying to control your gag reflex. A leader can dress immaculately, be well-versed, and say all the right things, and people can still see through their self-focused facade. If this leader took the time to read the room, they would see that their audience is not receptive to their message. This is because this leader never focused on developing charismatic communication skills.

On the other side of the spectrum, a charismatic leader can earn a tremendous amount of respect in only a few seconds. Upon first entering the room, she walks in, makes eye contact, leans into every conversation, and truly listens. She asks genuine questions to get to know the other person better, all without the intention of selfish gain.

Terri shares a few practical tips that help her stay people-focused and charismatic.

## Set a Daily Intention

Terri has realized that every time she inserts herself into a situation, and it becomes more about her than about the other person, she burns someone. That darn ego and pride seem to come out of nowhere, and they are killers. To keep herself accountable, Terri prays every morning. For others, it may be meditation or deep self-reflection.

## Apologize

If Terri starts acting like it's "all about me," she changes course very quickly. If she falters, she goes back and apologizes. Once, she apologized to a group of twenty people. When she realized what she was doing, she stopped in the middle of the presentation and said,

> Wait. Let me apologize. This is not about me. This is about *us* as a group and what *we* want as a group, not about what I want. If you don't mind forgiving me, let's start again. Where do you want to go with this? What do you want to do?

The apology sometimes is not for the other person. Instead, it's to remind herself to humble herself once again. Whether the other person accepts the apology or not, she's grateful for the lesson in humility.

## Have Accountability

Terri has trusted friends and support people who can provide accountability and get her back on track when she becomes self-focused. "We all need people who can point out our weaknesses and shortcomings, who can kick us in the butt if we get self-focused and make it all about us," she says. "We need someone who doesn't wait until we crash and burn to tell us about our faults."

Having accountability helps ensure you don't go on autopilot and revert to your old habits of communication. During times of unusual crises, it's easy to go back to old patterns of communication. In times of unusual chaos, it's easy to start treating people like problems and forget about their stories. That's why intentional accountability can help you stay on track.

## DEVELOP HUMILITY

An effective and charismatic leader must learn to let go of their own pride and recognize the validity of others' perspectives. For example, Terri's subordinate, who didn't get coverage for her class, perceived Terri as uncaring. At first, Terri thought this teacher's perspective was completely unfounded. But over time, she realized that her own brusque "get 'er done" personality, combined with the teacher's own traumatic past, was creating a very real perception. Rather than invalidating that perception, Terri needed to humbly accept other people's perspectives.

To that teacher at that moment, the perception was reality. Terri's mom reminded her, "People's perception is their truth. It may not be based on fact, but it's their truth, so you have to deal with their truth, even if it is not your truth." You can insist on the facts until you're blue in the face, but it won't help. The other person's perception is the reality of how they experience you, so you must take their perception seriously. Have the humility to recognize that your perspective may not always be right, either. Your vision of a situation may be colored by your own past as well.

Over the years, it has not been easy for Terri to swallow her pride. Yet the dividends have been huge. She has served in a state-level political position, where she regularly had to work a room. In this role, she frequently used the lessons she's learned about humbling herself and exercising restraint. People perceive her as a kind leader who will truly represent the people. They see her as approachable—someone who is easy to share concerns with across the board. Her humbling experiences have formed her into the leader and woman she is today.

As a leader, humility is one of the most important lessons you can learn. Former superintendent Ethan Fernandez says that you must avoid projecting a persona that communicates, "I'm the leader, I have it all put together. In my world, it's perfect. I don't ever make mistakes." That false front doesn't help you become a better leader.[8] Admitting your mistakes and weaknesses is what actually develops your strengths and helps you become better at what you do. Being able to admit when you make a mistake or have a particular weakness is what helps you grow.

When interviewing for a leadership position, one of the classic questions is, "Can you describe a couple of your strengths, and then, can you talk about a few of your weaknesses?" Ethan has never had a problem saying, "I'm weak in a specific area, but I'm going to work and strive to become better at developing that and eventually make that one of my strengths."

It's good to admit weaknesses and areas where you need growth. After all, isn't that the behavior that we want to model for our families, community, staff, and children? Ethan has often been willing to stand up in a staff meeting and openly say, "Hey, my bad, my mistake, I was wrong on this. We should have probably done it this way or that way. You were right when you said this, Mrs. So and so, my apologies." Public humility is one of the most important keys to being a charismatic leader.

Terri now considers herself skilled at working a crowd, whether it's made up of board members, parents, politicians, or kids. Like Terri, your ability to work a crowd needs to stem from humility rather than arrogance. Every administrator will come to a place where they will be humbled. These humbling, difficult experiences serve as an important catalyst - they provide the push leaders need to grow, mature, and elevate their leadership skills.

## DEVELOP COMMUNICATION SKILLS

It's easy to think that once you get to a top position, communication will be easy. Perhaps you imagine your subordinates jumping to obey your commands. But that's not reality. In top leadership, you have to work even harder to exercise restraint when someone else is wrong but doesn't realize it. You have to stop talking, you have to listen, and you have to understand where they're going. You have to learn to present another side without putting yourself in the middle of it.

The more your position rises, the more your communication skills must be elevated. Bryson, the lieutenant colonel we met in chapter one, explains that a former professor of the war college he attended used to say, "Physics doesn't move mountains. Chemistry does."[9] It's true. In order to read the room and influence those around you, you have to have great communication skills that will help you connect with others.

Communication or a lack of communication can truly make or break a leader's success. What you say and how you say it must never be overlooked.

Your conversation skills can make or break people's perceptions of you as a leader. A lot of times, your reputation precedes you as a leader, for better or for worse. People's perceptions of you as a leader are frequently formed by how you communicate with them.

Facilitating tough conversations is a specific skill set that leaders often don't feel confident handling. Whether addressing a deficiency in a subordinate or working through a disagreement, these conversations take art, practice, and confidence. Leaders can lose sleep at night over conflicts. All night, they toss and turn with their restless thoughts: "Oh man, I'm going to have to talk to him tomorrow!" These conversations are tough, and they're one of the worst parts of the job. But no matter how much we try to wish them away, these tough conversations are unavoidable.

Miles West is a military leader who understands how important communication skills are, especially in tough and stressful situations. As the chief officer of a large container ship that supplies military equipment around the world, Miles serves as the vessel's security officer. He's the on-scene commander during medical emergencies and responsible for twenty-three lives, not to mention the cargo. Exposed to the fury of Mother Nature, Miles faces the dangers of fire and flooding. In such a dangerous work environment, there is no room for miscommunication and miscalculations.

For Miles, the consequences of miscommunication can be dire. If the subordinate closes the wrong valve, the ship will flood. The entire crew will be fighting for their lives. Since his team's survival is directly dependent on his ability to communicate, Miles has an inherent motivation to be clear and to confirm that his communication has been understood and completed. Miles shares a few tips for "communicating as if your life depended on it."

## Be Clear and Concise

Miles says that whenever possible, you should keep thoughts and objectives organized, putting them in writing. Clearly explain what the team needs to accomplish. Be thoughtful of who your audience is and whether or not your message is coming across accurately and being understood and received. Have a two-way conversation with back-and-forth to ensure there is clarity.

Furthermore, keep your communication concise. On his ship, Miles often communicates via radio. Radios are used in passing arrangements from ship to ship or in anchoring operations on board the ship itself. When communicating via radio, concise communication is important. In the same way, when choosing what to say, sometimes less is more. Too many words can be confusing. Ask yourself, "What do you really want the other person to know? How could you get that information to them most effectively? What are the absolute essential keys that need to be said in order to keep everyone safe and moving forward?" Keep it short.

## Be Prepared When You Can

It's easiest to succeed in conflict situations when you have time to prepare for the conversation and rehearse it in advance. You have time to develop an outline, write it out, and decide where you want the conversation to go. If you have access to the documents that describe the baseline agreement between employer and employees, such as union contracts, familiarize yourself with them.

It's important not to dive right into a conversation and shoot from the hip without understanding what grounds the person you're speaking to has for their concern. Being familiar with the union content will help you be prepared for every angle that this conversation may take. It will ultimately protect you as a leader.

## Be Flexible

But there are times when these conversations can't be rehearsed. Under emergency circumstances or dire conditions, the communication must be issued right away. How do you prepare when you really can't rehearse what you'll be talking about with the person on the other side of the table?

Imagine this scenario. You are going about your business, doing your daily job. Then suddenly, you get sideswiped by a conflict or a difficult conversation with an employee. Because you haven't had a chance to prepare, you're scrambling to say the right things.

Having a difficult conversation without being able to rehearse it is always hard. You're trying to tread carefully and understand what they are saying: *What do we know? What is the problem? How can we find a solution?*

During these tough situations, rely on the wisdom and experience you have developed. As always, keep your words respectful and give the person your full attention. As in any communication situation, affirm the other person's concerns. And it's always wise to try to buy yourself some time: "Listen, I hear what you're saying, and even if I can't find a solution right this minute, let me think about it and we'll get back together and find a solution to this problem."

Even in these unexpected situations, take a moment for self-care. Even if you only have ten seconds, focus on intentionally pausing, breathing, and thinking about how to treat the other person with respect. Otherwise, your rapid-fire anxiety will get the best of you, leading to an outcome that's not desirable for either the leader or the person on the receiving end of the conversation.

This emergency self-care will be much easier if you've been taking regular time for self-care during the week. The more rested you are, the less frantic you will become when the stress is overwhelming. Rest and self-care will help you avoid rude, disrespectful, one-way firing because you're unprepared. The more you've taken care of yourself, the less likely it is that the anxiety of this unplanned situation will throw you for a loop.

## Be Respectful

It all comes back to the core value of respect. Respect will always get you through the conversation of conflict that can't be rehearsed. An effective communicator never gets disrespectful in any way. When you're having a tough conversation, make sure the subordinate feels heard. Repeat what they said and make sure you understand the problem. Then, assess the situation - compile what you know, identify the core issue, and determine a solution.

Always be professional and make sure that person is being heard. Try to ensure that you and your conversation partner both walk away from that conversation feeling like neither of you has lost—that you have both have won some mutual understanding.

There are times that you won't be able to accommodate another person's point of view, but you must maintain respect anyway. At times, you as a leader must simply make a decision: "You may agree or disagree, but trust me, follow my lead. At the end of the day, this is the way we're going to go." As a leader, there are times when your communication must be very direct and immediate. But even in this decision-making process, you can maintain an attitude of respect and care.

To finish out this chapter on charismatic leadership, let's listen to a story from Brian T. Miller, a principal from Montana. Brian learned in an unexpected way what it really means to lead with compassion. Early in his life, shortly after becoming married, Brian ran a group home of teenagers out of Philadelphia. Some of the six teen boys in their home had recently come out of the juvenile system and were transitioning to freedom. Others were staying in the group home as their last chance before going into the juvenile system.[10]

One student in particular was incredibly challenging. J. C. came from a very rough neighborhood in Philadelphia. This boy would be in Brian's face every night, cursing him out, spitting in his face, and trying to get him to fight. J. C. was a scary, scary kid.

One day, Brian's grandmother wanted to come visit him. She was a very pure, sweet woman who was only four feet tall.

Brian tried to dissuade her: "These kids are going to freak you out. Don't come." But Grandma insisted on coming. One day, while she was visiting,

Brian was out doing yard work. Suddenly, he realized that both J. C. and his grandmother had gone missing.

"Oh no! This is not good," Brian worried.

He went inside to find his grandmother sitting at the table, holding J. C.'s hands. The boy was reading one of his rap songs to her. It was littered with profanity, violence, and sexuality. Yet she was holding his hand and crying as he read the lyrics.

"Because of my upbringing, I can relate to you," Grandma told J. C.

J. C. instantly developed immense respect for Brian's grandmother. Before Grandma left, Brian took a photo of the two of them arm in arm, big smiles on their faces. Even after she left, Grandma and J. C. maintained a mutual relationship, writing back and forth for the next year.

From that moment on, Brian changed the way he approached J. C. From his grandma, he realized that true leaders can momentarily set aside their own convictions to listen to someone else's story. Grandma herself would never talk that way or let her kids talk that way. But she put all that on the shelf so she could see J. C. and truly enter his world. When Brian started to engage with J. C. in the same way, their relationship grew. Even now, fifteen years later, J. C. and Brian still FaceTime each other occasionally.

Brian's grandmother communicated to J. C., "I'm going to choose you over me." Instead of being self-focused, she chose to build this relationship. This is the key to charismatic leadership. A leader must always choose the other person. Set aside your own ego, enjoy your subordinates, and care about those you lead. Get beyond the accusatory words that the struggling person is saying and really hear the person. See their struggles. Find out their needs. Get rid of your own agendas and your own pride, and really see the person in front of you. Only then will you be able to read the room to lead the room.

## AIR TRAFFIC CONTROL

The most polished school and district leaders can read the room. It's one of the most important skills that administrators can develop. When you've done your research, know what's on the table, and understand the stories of your listeners, you'll be prepared for what's ahead. You will avoid using communication strategies that don't work with those individuals. You will watch your audience and pick up on subtle information about how they are responding. Like a pilot reading their instruments, you will keep close tabs on your environment so you can position yourself for maximum success.

- Learn people's stories. Reading the room means understanding others' stories. Taking the time to understand where others are coming from will pay long-term dividends.

- Practice self-reflection. You can't effectively lead others if you're not leading yourself. Be aware of the times when your own self-focus is getting in the way.
- Be a charismatic, connected leader. A charismatic leader isn't just focused on outcomes and numbers. This leader connects with others on a personal basis and builds trust. The focus of a charismatic leader is always on others.
- Develop humility. A charismatic, connected leader is willing to see other people's perspectives. This leader avoids arrogance and allows circumstances to teach them humility.
- Practice good communication skills. Preparation, flexibility, and respect will help you stay in touch with the people you lead, especially during tough conversations.

**NOTES**

1. "Basic Instrument Reading PA28," *Flight Level*. Accessed December 15, 2022, https://flightlevel.com.hk/pages/1_flight_basic.html.

2. Matthew Cox, "F-35 Pilot Killed in April Crash May Have Ignored Aircraft Instruments: Selva," June 19, 2019. Accessed December 15, 2022, https://www.military.com/daily-news/2019/06/19/f-35-pilot-killed-april-crash-may-have-ignored-aircraft-instruments-selva.html.

3. "The Six Pack: Basic Flight Instruments," *Pilot Institute*, December 6, 2021. Accessed December 15, 2022, https://pilotinstitute.com/six-pack-instruments/.

4. Terri Rufert (retired superintendent), in discussion with the author, November 8, 2022.

5. Brian Miller (principal), in discussion with the author, August 31, 2022.

6. Shonna Waters, PhD, "How to Tap into Heart and Soul to Lead with More Charisma," last modified November 30, 2021. Accessed February 28, 2023, https://www.betterup.com/blog/charismatic-leadership.

7. Waters, "How to Tap into Heart and Soul."

8. Retired superintendent #1, in discussion with the author, October 5, 2022. Name changed for privacy.

9. Retired colonel, in discussion with the author, August 12, 2022. Name changed for privacy.

10. Brian Miller (principal), in discussion with the author, August 31, 2022.

*Chapter 5*

# Inflow and Outflow

## *Hiring and Firing with Dignity*

A dome of blue sky stretches above the cockpit window, and the pilot gazes dreamily at the white streaks of contrails crisscrossing the sky, the remnants of other airplanes in flight. To a pilot, those lines mean one thing: job security. Those white streaks are proof that air travelers are still adventuring to their next destinations. These streaks show that our economy is taking off again after the worldwide crisis that led to decreased air travel.

But to an airplane mechanic, these condensation trails mean something else altogether. The trails are caused by the airplane's exhaust system and air inlet system. Air is drawn into the engine and used for combustion; then the byproducts are expelled in the rear of the plane, forming the contrails.[1] The air intake and exhaust systems ensure the safety, power, and efficiency of the flight.[2]

Just like the intake and outtake of an airplane are important in flight, the intake and outtake of employees help ensure the safety, power, and efficiency of a company, school, or district. It's important to "intake" the correct employees and then wisely let go of the ones who need to move on.

This isn't an easy process. Leaders are faced with the pressure of hiring the right people and also making the decision to fire an employee who ends up being not a good fit. Acorn Welding notes that airplane "exhaust systems undergo a lot of stress and strain throughout their lifecycle because they have a tough job."[3] In the same way, hiring and firing is a tough job, and it's one that's unavoidable.

There are a lot of things that can go wrong with the exhaust system. If the combustion byproducts are not properly expelled, carbon monoxide poisoning or fire can result.[4] The engine's functionality can be reduced, or the exhaust can "interfere with the aerodynamics or disturb the airflow" around the plane's engines.[5]

In the same way, hiring or firing the wrong people in the wrong way can interfere with the overall goal, direction, and stability of your organization. An airplane needs "flow dynamics [to] help determine how the gases will flow through the exhaust system and how pressure will be handled," and the flow dynamics depend on the unique needs of your individual exhaust system.[6] In the same way, your organization needs flow dynamics that contribute to the safety and stability of your district or company.

How can you do better at creating an efficient "flow" within your organization? How can you improve at handling the necessary pressure? How can you come up with a unique model of hiring and firing that fits the unique needs of your organization?

## HIRING

When hiring new staff for your district, you are faced with many decisions. Do you hire from within the district, selecting trusted staff members who have been groomed with the district's vision, mission, philosophy, and core values? Or do you pick outsiders with fresh, external ideas? The answer can be complex, and it depends on the specific needs of the position you're hiring for.

If you are hiring a staff member for a position that requires high levels of trust and experience, you should consider hiring from within. If you need a new assistant superintendent, you might choose that trustworthy, wise HR guy who's been in the district for twenty-six years. He's going to help your team because he has a lot of historical knowledge of the district. For such a high-stakes leadership position, you will likely need a trusted member of the district who is willing to learn and change and adapt as needed. A person like this can be a very valuable contribution to your team.

On the other hand, let's say you're hiring a new staff member for your department of diversity, equity, and inclusion. In this situation, you might pick someone who has recently arrived in the district. This person has some knowledge of the district but also has fresh, external ideas. They can give you a completely different way of thinking, which is very valuable. This may be a value-added asset for this position. You need someone with fresh ideas who can give you a completely different lens to see equity.

Or perhaps you need to hire someone for a position that has become so ingrown that there is a history of people quitting. As you consider this role, how can you adapt your flow dynamics? You may want to choose someone from outside. You'll need a completely fresh perspective. You find an external hire who isn't embroiled in the messy internal dynamics. This person can come in and disrupt the status quo. They need to be strong enough to make decisions, even when there is a lot of pushback.

Whom you hire depends on the needs of the position. Do you need to establish trust? A complete disruption of what's in place? A new perspective? As you do your rounds, try to think about what you need in each department. Where do you need fresh eyes, and where do you need consistency? When you hire, look for strong leaders who are willing to learn, people who are strong in their convictions, and staff who are willing to listen and adapt.

There are times when the needs of your organization require extreme action. You may have been directed to bring in new blood, or you may have made the decision yourself. Regardless of the circumstances, there is definitely an art to firing, which is usually not popular content to cover in professional development and credential programs.

## FIRING

The task of firing or letting go of an employee comes easier for some leaders than for others. Your comfort level with firing is usually based on your past experiences, the confidence that you have in yourself as a leader, and most definitely union relations. This task often requires rehearsal and coaching from people who are not associated with your organization.

Firing a difficult employee is an art. A lot of thought and time must be spent on developing an exit plan for the employee, no matter the circumstances. A leader must learn to release employees with compassion and in a way that preserves their dignity.

Sometimes, this empathy and compassion are learned the hard way—through a leader's own experience of being fired. Superintendent Carl Gomez's difficult experience of being unfairly fired gave him a new sensitivity toward the people in his current district. It has informed his own approach as a leader when he hires and fires.

Carl recently shared a phenomenal story about the courage and perspective he gained through his own experience of being fired.[7] Before he was a superintendent, Carl was a high school principal at a school in his hometown. He'd been brought back home to try to resurrect a dying school, and in just three years, the school went from very low performing to very high ranking. His school became one of the highest-achieving schools in the entire state. It was nothing short of phenomenal.

Because of his success, Carl was given the possibility of becoming the superintendent of his hometown school district. Carl was elated. Not only would he be promoted, but he would have the opportunity to continue to pour into the students of his hometown. "Those are *my kids*," he explained affectionately. "We've invested in each other. We're growing."

Carl was looking forward to stepping into the position of superintendent. Things were going well, and Carl had no reason to expect that anything was going wrong. But out of nowhere, a member of the conservatorship made a false accusation to get rid of him. In some parts of the country, conservators oversee the operations of the district and can direct the action of a campus principal, superintendent, or board of trustees. This includes termination.

One day, the conservatorship brought Carl into the office. They were the ones who were responsible for the superintendent search, and they gave Carl a solid evaluation: 3.6 out of 4. But then Joe, the member who had made a false accusation, dropped a bomb on Carl.

"I want you to know we decided to go a different direction," he said. "I'm depending on you to get the community on board with our new direction."

Carl was reeling from the news, but he knew it was not his responsibility to get the community on board. He replied with confidence, "That's not my job; that's your job. If you hire someone else, it's your job to get the community on board."

Joe was not pleased. On several occasions, he sent the school board's attorney to ask Carl to play ball. But Carl would not play the game.

"I am not going to do anything malicious, because I love my kids," Carl told the attorney. "But I know it's not my job to engraft the new leader into the community. That's a decision you all made, knowing it was in the best interest of our community."

Joe was angered by Carl's assertiveness, and he concocted a plan to say that Carl stole time as a principal. Not only did he keep him out of the superintendency, but he also fired him from his high school principalship. Joe wouldn't go to court because he knew he would have to lie in court. He knew his claims were bogus. But nonetheless, Carl was fired. His career was turned upside down.

At the deposition, Joe admitted that Carl stole nothing; he reported to the state department that Carl worked fifty-nine out of sixty days. So to say that Carl was missing work was just a bogus reason to get him out. However, Joe, being in a position of power, did exactly that.

Carl's experience of being unfairly fired gave him a new sensitivity toward the people in his district and informed his own approaches as a leader. "Because of what has happened to me, I have the simplest hiring and firing process," he explained. He chuckled as he said, "We have this whole sheet of procedures for hiring and firing. I don't care anything about it. I have three things I'm looking for every time: knowledge, skill, and attitude."

Carl knows that attitude is the most important of the three. If a staff member has a flexible attitude and wants to learn and grow, he is patient with their lack of knowledge and skill. When he first came to his current school district, several staff members were serving in illegal positions as "classified teachers." Rather than firing them because they didn't have appropriate training, Carl looked for a way to grow his own leaders.

Carl knew these teachers were good people who simply didn't have qualifications yet. He wanted to do his best to work with them. He made it clear to his employees that if they really wanted to work with him and were willing to grow, he would be very patient and accommodating.

On the other hand, he was strict with teachers who had a bad attitude. He knew the gaps in teachers' knowledge and skill areas could be remedied through professional development. But if an employee had a bad attitude, that couldn't be trained out of them—it was the individual's choice.

As he took over the leadership in his district, Carl simply asked his employees, "Do you want to be here? Do you want to be better? I'll pay for your practice training. I'll pay for your practice test. We'll work with our local university to get you back in school. We'll do the whole nine yards." Then he dropped the bomb. "I can help you with knowledge, I can help you with skill, but I cannot help you with your attitude. And if you're going to have a bad attitude, I'm going to fire you. Point blank period."

"I believe in the talent of my team," Carl explained. Only the teachers who weren't willing to work with him would be let go. As a result, all of the teachers in Carl's district are now 100 percent certified and appropriately placed.

Carl's termination experience greatly impacted his leadership approach to hiring and firing. Because his own termination was based on lies and unfounded evidence, he learned to focus on ensuring dignity and honor for those in his care. And you can do the same.

So exactly how do you, as a leader, make employment decisions in dignified ways? Let's learn a bit more about the process and the practical ways that will help you ensure honesty and fairness for those you serve.

## HIRING AND FIRING WITH DIGNITY

First, let's define our terms. *Hiring with dignity* means looking beyond just the person's qualifications and truly hiring for character and heart. And *firing with dignity* means understanding that this person still has character and heart but may not be a good fit for *this* position.

When you hire and fire with dignity, you are leaning in. You are truly approaching the situation as if you were the one being hired or fired. Remember that being hired or being fired will significantly change the course of your employee's career and will most definitely be a memorable experience. So you must approach these decisions with utmost care and wisdom.

It's important to be personally involved with the firing process from the start. Don't just wipe your hands clean. Don't leave all the legwork to the HR department without ensuring that the organization is taking the classy avenue.

When making these important decisions, be personally invested in the outcome for the employee. Remember that your actions could permanently impact the public perception of the individual you are firing. Are you contributing to public harm, or are you protecting people who deserve it? Are you feeding the gossip train? Or are you ensuring your decisions are based on solid ground? And when you actually deliver the message, are you exhibiting compassion and love? Or are you cold and ruthless?

Perhaps you think that union and bargaining agreements make it impossible to fire with dignity. But dignity has nothing to do with union and bargaining agreements. Whether or not the district or school is bound to union processes has no impact on your ability to act with dignity. No matter the legal processes, it is absolutely possible and feasible for the leader to lead with heart and compassion.

You can absolutely make the decision to let go of an employee, which can be a very difficult and stressful situation, and still act from a place of love. Pay attention to your body language and tone of voice. Imagine yourself on the other side of the table.

There is much more to firing than hurrying through an HR checklist. Don't be tempted to cut corners or to take the easy way out by making rash, quick decisions. Instead, take the time to truly understand the magnitude of your decisions and how your approach will impact the person for years to come. Keep in mind that a rushed and unwarranted firing decision could also affect your own reputation and leadership success in the long run.

Hiring and firing with dignity must never be forgotten. Whether or not the employee is a good fit for your organization is not the only thing to consider. No matter what they may have done, you still owe it to them to ensure that mutual respect and compassion are demonstrated. That is the dignified approach.

## AIR TRAFFIC CONTROL

The intake and outtake of your organization are just as important as they are during flight.

- When hiring, keep in mind the unique needs of the position you are looking for. This ensures you get the right person for the right spot.
- When firing, remember to be honest and avoid power plays.
- Firing and hiring with dignity means keeping the best interest of the employee in mind, even when difficult decisions must be made.

## NOTES

1. "How Does an Aircraft Exhaust System Affect Engine Performance?," *Acorn Welding*, last modified May 26, 2020. Accessed March 1, 2023, https://www.acorn-welding.com/blog/post/aircraft-exhaust-system-affect-engine-performance/.

2. "How Does an Aircraft Exhaust System Affect Engine Performance?"

3. "What Is an Aircraft Exhaust System Analysis?" *Acorn Welding*. Accessed December 15, 2022, https://www.acornwelding.com/blog/post/what-aircraft-exhaust-system-analysis/.

4. "How Does an Aircraft Exhaust System Affect Engine Performance?"

5. Mike Berry, "Exhaust Essentials," last modified February 24, 2019. Accessed March 1, 2023, https://www.aviationsafetymagazine.com/aircraft/exhaust-essentials/.

6. "What Is an Aircraft Exhaust System Analysis?"

7. Superintendent #2, in discussion with the author, September 1, 2022. Name changed for privacy.

*Chapter 6*

# Wind Currents

## *The Push and Pull of Competing Agendas*

As the airplane continues to climb, it heads through the lower atmosphere. The airplane is flying into the wind, and the air flowing over the plane's wings provides the lift it needs to stay afloat. The strong headwind makes the flight easy but can slow the plane down.[1] A tailwind pushes the plane forward and helps the fuel burn.

In the lower atmosphere, wind swirls around buildings and trees, bouncing off in different directions. The push and pull of air currents surround the plane. These quick variations in wind speed create differing levels of lift, causing the plane to go up and down. It's typical turbulence. A natural part of flying. The pilot knows he doesn't need to fear the bumps.[2]

In the same way, it's normal to experience the push and pull in leadership. Leaders will work with many different people who have an insane number of demands and requests. Sometimes, those demands conflict with the mission or intent of the organization. A leader must know how to identify which issues are worth attending to and which are not worth prioritizing. A leader must learn how to pick their battles and go to war only when necessary.

Just like a passenger needs to learn that turbulence is normal while flying through the lower atmosphere, a leader needs to realize that bumps are a normal part of leadership. You don't need to fear the turbulence. (Even if you are a control freak that grips the seat and sweats bullets with every little bump in the air.)

Turbulence can show up in many ways. Superintendent Gerald White has experienced the push and pull of leadership, just like many other district leaders have. Gerald experienced it with an external contract: the transportation provider. The company didn't want to come down in pricing with him, so he let them walk away.[3] "Fine. We're done. We quit," the bus provider said, thinking Gerald wouldn't be able to find a new provider and expecting him to come crawling back to them in a few months. But Gerald scrambled to find a new transportation contractor, and he was successful. The push-and-pull dynamic was normal, and he didn't let it fluster him.

Another time, Gerald realized this same bus provider was overcharging his district numerous miles per day—$100,000 a year. He began withholding that money from their payments; the company was upset. Gerald stayed calm and, through a process, was able to recover all of the money that was lost. He got through the turbulence.

When difficulties arise, a leader needs to know how to navigate the push and pull of a wide variety of priorities—and do it all without panicking. If you are a leader who acts as if the roof is always on fire in every high-stress situation, it's truly a turn-off to staff. That's why it's so important to be prepared for some of the most common areas where normal turbulence can take place. One of those turbulent places is union negotiations.

## PUSH AND PULL OF UNION NEGOTIATIONS

Working effectively with union representation can be a very stressful undertaking that many leaders dread. However, when you let go of fear and tackle the turbulence, you can successfully navigate healthy and prosperous union relationships.

Dr. Bianca Cervantes is a living example of this. After thirty-nine years of experience in education, Cervantes knows a thing or two about the turbulence of negotiations. Let's learn a few of her top tips for surviving turbulence.

### Before Negotiation Day

Cervantes believes that successful union negotiations are less about shortcuts, tips, and tricks and more about building relationships.[4]

"Start early to build relationships so that you can deal with the push and pull effectively," she says. "Preparation for negotiations must begin right after the superintendent is appointed."

*Build the Relationship Right Away*

Immediately after being hired, you must hit the ground running. Get out there and start listening and learning from the troops. Learn everything you can about the district, their direction, and what they've been doing. From day one, purposefully develop relationships with the union president and the other officials.

Even when you don't like them, focus on developing a working relationship. "You don't have to take them home," Cervantes chuckles, "but you do have to develop a good working relationship." It starts early by getting to know them as human beings and vise versa.

## Create an Open Door Policy

Right away, set up regular and informal meetings with the president of the union so you can establish mutual understanding. Make sure the president has your cell number and knows very clearly that they can text, call, email, or drop into your office at any time.

Communicate, "If anything comes up, let me know. We will meet that very day, unless I'm out of the office. It's a high priority for me. We are going to problem-solve together." Rather than setting up regular meetings, which can easily develop into stiff formalities with nothing to talk about, give an open invitation for spur-of-the-moment meetings whenever the union president has a concern. Whenever possible, you will drop everything you're doing and address their problem immediately.

Once the union leaders have had a chance to test out your sincerity and you have proven you are available, they will feel a lot more comfortable. They will start feeling like they are part of the team that is focused on the students in the district.

You may be groaning, "Ugh, I don't want to hear it."

But Bianca explains how this is an easy gift that will bear exponential fruit later. "After all, you're not losing anything by giving them this access," she says. "Instead, you're letting them know they're important enough that they can contact you just like any of your administrators can."

## Listen

It's important to let union leaders know that you value them as people and that you value their leadership in the association. To show how important they are to you, make sure to ask them their opinions. Try to find a simple question that you can ask the union leader's opinion about. Then consider their opinions and incorporate them if necessary.

Listening is a low-hanging fruit that you can easily start with. Listen with intention. Value the union representative's opinion, and then ask them questions. "What does that look like? How do you think others would feel about that? Do you think that your members would agree with that?" When you begin to have those conversations, union leaders will begin to feel positive feelings about you. They'll realize, "Oh, they did listen to me!"

## Chapter 6

### Communicate Regularly

Be proactive about informing union representatives about upcoming issues. Do so before the issues hit the fan, before everybody else knows about them. If you have an issue brewing with a member of their association, say,

> I just want to let you know, I'm going to be dealing with this. I'm going to be listening to both sides of what happened. But if what I know right now proves to be true, this is the action that I'm likely to be taking.

Let them know in advance about the changes you're considering making and why. Invite them to do the same for you, to give you a heads-up. Encourage them to call you or text you to let you know what's brewing. When you develop that relationship early and meet with them often, you'll already know what they'll ask for when you get to the negotiating table.

If leaders have been proactive in building relationships, they will avoid making quick judgments in their minds:

"They won't understand."
"I don't agree with anything they have to say."

Without communication, a leader might be quick to anticipate or to misread certain statements and events, just because of the fear factor that's involved with the union. But when you really entrench yourself in that relationship-building process in advance, you might be surprised at the outcome.

Many leaders have said with surprise, "Wow, this process isn't as painful as I thought it would be. We do have a lot of agreements that are on the table." When leaders prioritize their relationship, they quickly realize that not only do they have a lot of agreements in place, but they kind of like each other.

Come together for the organizations success'. Take initiative, show kindness, and be grateful for your union partners. Keep the conversation focused on what is best for the team. If you remember that it's always about the collective goals, not about your feelings, it can be a very healthy conversation.

### Negotiation Day

You've prepared, you've built relationships, and you've done all you can. With this infrastructure in place, there are times when negotiation day goes very smoothly. But at other times, the union makes unrealistic requests and even sometimes relentless demands. When it appears to be an uphill battle to reach agreements, leaders must be wise in handling the back-and-forth of union collective bargaining. There's a high demand revolving around compensation. It's pretty steep and can sometimes be unrealistic from the leader's perspective. Here are some ideas that can help.

## Have Realistic Expectations

It's important to remember that negotiations are just that: negotiations. If you're going to buy a car, you expect to negotiate. You never assume that you'll offer a low price, and the salesperson will immediately say, "Wonderful, here's your car." It doesn't happen that way. You expect a back-and-forth.

The same happens in union negotiations. It's important to know that both sides will start out at the extremes and work toward the middle. Where you start is not where you're going to end. Go into that calmly, knowing this is the process. We're going to start out at extremes and negotiate until both entities get to the point where we can agree. At the end of the day, we will eventually agree.

## Be Prepared

When it comes to union negotiations, there is no substitute for preparation. A lack of preparation can lead to disastrous outcomes. You must be well prepared in advance. You may think, "My negotiations are not until December." But your union president may pop in at the beginning of September and say, "What do you think about this topic we're discussing?" And you must be prepared to respond. If you're not prepared for that particular question, it's okay to say, "I don't know the answer right now, but I will talk to whomever I need to talk to and get you the answer."

## Know Your Contract

Going into a negotiation, it's important to know your contract inside and out. Be able to cite it: "In this section, this article, it refers to this." The more you know it, the more confident the union members are going to be that you're following it.

Your administrators also need to know the contract inside and out. There's no excuse for any administrator to not know the contract. That should be a priority that all superintendents have for their administrators.

## Know Your Budget

Know where you stand at all times and how much wiggle room you do or don't have. Discuss the budget openly and often, both at board meetings and at staff meetings, making sure there is an abundance of opportunities when the budget is discussed.

This way, there won't be any surprises. That transparency is critical. George Brad, a columnist who wrote for Forbes, called it "fearless transparency." What an amazing term! Be open and fearlessly transparent.

*Look for Low-Hanging Fruit*

As you're headed into negotiations—just like when establishing a relationship—look for the easy wins and low-hanging fruit. Set a tone that says you are willing to compromise and give. Have those discussions. Those informal and formal meetings will give you an idea of what the demands are going to be.

*Keep Your Ears to the Ground*

The other piece critical piece is to keep your collective administrative ears to the ground so the demands are not a surprise. Talk to your site leaders. "What are you hearing? What do you think? What are some of the issues that are happening at the site level that we are likely to see at the bargaining table?" If you are paying attention, there shouldn't be any surprises.

*Model Respectful Debate*

You are the leader. You set the tone—there's no question about it. Even when the union representatives say the most derogatory things, you can just sit there and go, "Hmm. OK." And just continue. You, as a leader, must have a course planned, and you must continue on that course. Don't allow other things to distract you or upset you.

Bianca says that she warns her team in advance: "If you see me just taking notes and not really commenting a lot, it's because I'm trying not to say something that would make it worse." Do not allow that disrespect to distract you from your focus. Just let the conversation come back to where it was supposed to be.

When someone says something cynical or attacking, stay focused. Simply state, "That's not the way we're going to go." Even when talking to people you dislike, find that medium spot where you understand their agenda and they understand your agenda. Find some middle ground and a collaborative way to move forward. Build healthy partnerships that can lead to productive conversations and a focus on what is truly important.

*Keep Your Focus on Students*

Sometimes, as leaders, your ego and pride become the forefront instead of the students' needs. You feel defensive, get offended, and take things personally. *"How dare they do this to me?"*

But this process is not about any individual adult. It is about the students and the staff collectively as a district. When a leader storms out in the middle of negotiations or there is a back-and-forth battle with words that contributes to a very toxic and disrespectful negotiation culture, it shows that the negotiation has become all about the leader.

The leader is no longer focused on the right thing: educating students.

It's important to help the union leaders feel the shared weight of responsibility for the task of educating kids. Make them feel responsible for the fiscal health of the organization, not just for their own salaries. They need to have ownership. If the school district is not fiscally healthy, it will start losing jobs. If the district is overspending to please the union, it will have to cut somewhere, and kids will be affected. Since personnel costs make up the biggest part of the budget, overspending will eventually hurt staffing as well. Help bring the focus back to the kids and the health of the district.

## Remain Hopeful

Even if relationships seem toxic, change is always possible. Bianca shared a situation of amazing transformation that took place in her relationship with the union representatives in her district. The relationships were very toxic, and it was clear they didn't like each other. One day, Bianca sat down with her chief of human resources and discussed the situation.

"Should we try this reconciliation and relationships training?" HR asked.

Bianca responded, "Why not? I don't know what else we can do. We've tried all these different strategies and nothing seems to work. What do we have to lose?"

They didn't have anything to lose, but Bianca dreaded the painful ride to the event and back with the union representatives. Sure enough, riding in the van was torture for Bianca. There were representatives, administrators, district and site leaders, and representatives from classified and teachers' associations. It was as uncomfortable for them as it was for her. There was a lot of toxicity in the van, and they could all feel it. But they pushed through the discomfort and arrived at the training.

During the training, Bianca was listening to a district superintendent talk about his previous experience with union relations.

"The union was calling for the board to fire me," he said.

> The teacher association president actually spoke at a board meeting and asked that they remove me as superintendent. Yet we went through this process of reconciliation and really started setting up structures and protocols for collaboration and discussion. We started having regular meetings, getting to know each other, and developing relationships. It is a miracle.

Bianca sat there listening to this man and thought, "He's talking about me. If I had a diary, I would think he was reading it."

Bianca did not realize that other leaders in the room were feeling the same way. Directly in front of her were some of the most toxic people she knew. These people did not like her, and she was not crazy about them either. They were all sitting there, listening, when suddenly, one of them reached across the round table and said, "Why don't we do this?"

Each member of the different associations agreed: "Yes, I'm tired of the way things are."

Bianca just about fell out of her chair. "Hallelujah. I cannot believe this," she thought. Out loud, she said, "We are tired, too."

Then the dialogue began. Bianca and her district started sending teams to the regional training. They set up the protocols and started having meetings. During the training, instead of problem-solving fictional situations as a practice, they decided to dig into their real problems.

The problem-solving strategies worked. A few years later, when they faced challenges associated with the COVID pandemic (and every leader knows how extremely painful that was), Bianca's district already had relationships in place. The district and the union proved they had the foundation necessary to work together during really tough situations without losing their collaboration focus.

One night, during the onset of the pandemic, Bianca's leadership team was meeting at ten p.m. Bianca was on a conference call with her administrators, discussing closing the schools. They had a professional development day scheduled for the next day, and they were rearranging their whole agenda to accommodate the reality of the pandemic.

During the meeting, Bianca got a call from the union president. She took the call immediately.

"You know, Bianca, I think we're going to need to . . ." the president began.

"I'm on the phone with all these people right now," Bianca said, "and we are changing it right now. I have a Google Doc, so you can go in there and see what the changes are." She also notified the president of the classified association and had her start looking at the spreadsheet, too.

The union leader had no idea Bianca and her team would be meeting at ten o'clock at night in order to come up with a reasonable plan. Bianca and the union leader continued to work in partnership through the most stressful times.

This story shows the power of working together with your union representatives. Bianca was at her wits' end, but this training changed things. She worked through a complete transformation of culture.

It wasn't just a superficial change, where they labeled things differently but kept doing things the way they always had. They really changed things deep down. That's why Bianca is now such a powerful advocate for working together in the push and pull of negotiation. This difficult experience taught lifelong lessons that benefited Bianca's leadership skills for the long term.

## PUSH AND PULL OF THE SCHOOL BOARD

As a superintendent, you may very likely, at some point in your career, face something even more daunting than communicating with the union: dealing with the push and pull of the school board. Governance teams have demonstrated that they can sometimes be messy, non-cohesive, and full of competing agendas.

Communicating with the school board is intimidating because they are typically the only group that can actually hire and fire a superintendent. Even if the leader has a rock-solid contract with severance built in, it can be terrifying to work with school boards. If just one school board member goes rogue and starts recruiting the other board members or a new board election brings in new personal agendas, the superintendent could be toast. We see this happening throughout public education.

Communicating with the board of directors can be a challenge. Most school board members, even those whose hearts are in the right place, do not speak education. They typically do not understand the issues that superintendents, administrators, and teachers look at every day. This is one of the biggest frustrations for administrators. School board members are your bosses, and they really don't know much about the day in and day out of working in a school. How does a superintendent work through those times?

### Be Communicative

Even though the school board may not understand the world you live in, you can do your best to help them get a window into your everyday educational experience. Bianca Cervantes says that connecting with the school board goes back to the theme of communication.

Communication can include mid-year meetings with the school board that lay out the road map of where the district is going. Periodic academic achievement reports can provide data presentations and spotlight different schools within the district. A mid-year work study can allow you to revamp the original road map if necessary. These suggestions come from Ava Reyes, a leader who speaks from the perspective of both a site administrator and a school board member for another district. Since she wears both hats, she's an expert on the needs of school boards and leadership.

Ava explains that during these regular meetings, administrators can present new initiatives they are considering. These meetings allow them to get a strong pulse of the school board. Is the school board excited, hesitant, oppositional, or does it just need more information? Regular communication can solve these dilemmas before they become problematic.[5]

From the beginning, be honest always, even when it's easier not to be. When you don't want to tell them things, do it anyway. They don't want to hear it, but they have to hear it. It's a matter of keeping the board informed.

**Coach the Board**

Bianca strongly believes that the superintendent should take responsibility for educating the board.

"You are the teacher," Bianca tells superintendents.

> You're the one that needs to make sure you lay things out so they can truly understand the budget, so they can truly understand where we're at, why the association is requesting what they're requesting. So you're always keeping them constantly informed, whether in open session, closed session, through personal one-on-one phone calls, texts, or email.

A superintendent has the responsibility to ensure her school board is up to speed with the process of district negotiations. This leader must do their best to ensure that the school board is kept informed of union requests. They must work to ensure the board supports her recommendations for a negotiation settlement. The school board must be kept up to speed with the ins and outs of what is going on in multiple conversations with multiple priorities. Communication and transparency with the board help ensure that the superintendent is successful, not just now, but in the long term.

Ava explains that sometimes you, as a superintendent, must do a lot of damage control in getting the board to behave in a certain way. Do training behind the scenes. Provide guidance to the school board: "Please don't say that during the board meeting" or "I would suggest you rephrase it to be something like this."

When controversy or conflict is anticipated, prepare and review a script with the board president and have talking points for the entire board. The better they look before the public, the better the district and the leadership look as well. Develop, prepare, and protect your team.

With communication and coaching, a board and superintendent can work with one another despite differences. You can become a well-oiled machine. Even when disagreements come up, you can handle them appropriately and professionally. You can work together to try to make the best decision that you all feel the most comfortable with.

When you communicate with and coach the board, you will come together with one voice. You will show the community that the board is unified—even when there are varying opinions that can lead to strong disagreements. When it comes time to present publicly, it's critical to demonstrate solidarity—despite any differences behind the scenes, you must put on a united front.

## Put the Ball in the School Board's Court

When it's showtime, there are a few tactics to keep in mind that will help the meeting go smoothly. One is to put the responsibility on the board when there are disagreements. The superintendent can say to the school board, "These are the options. How would you like for me to proceed?"

Putting the ball in the school board's court empowers the school board members. They feel like they are equipped to make a decision. They are grateful that the administrator is looking to them for guidance to move forward. In large-scale conflict, this type of approach gets the responsibility off the superintendent's shoulders. The community members who are watching the meeting will stop blaming the superintendent and will realize, "This is what the board will enforce."

## Be Knowledgeable

A superintendent needs to be able to answer almost every question the board may ask. When they ask specific questions:

> "Have you as the superintendent sought out legal
> counsel in a particular circumstance?"
> "What are the options we have as a board?"
> "What can we do about this situation?"
> "What will the repercussions be?"

You must be able to fire back, "I already checked with legal counsel, did that background check, got this report, this person followed up with me, etc.." Your knowledge will give you credibility. You will gain the board's confidence. Without this confidence in the superintendent, unity falls apart very quickly.

If a superintendent doesn't do his or her homework and isn't ready to answer the board, the board becomes disorganized while waiting to hear back. Come as close as you can to knowing everything possible. Know the specific numbers of grants, budget, facilities, education code, anything. The most impressive superintendents are always able to come up with the answer to a wide variety of questions. At a minimum, they can efficiently find the answer upon request.

In addition, try to be aware of any employee, student, staff member, or parent that might come forward with objections for the board. Forewarn the board: "Hey, a parent might come forward today and say XYZ. But this is what we know to be true, this is what was investigated." When superintendents are confident and in touch with their school and their district, the board feels like they're getting the information they need to make decisions.

**Utilize Closed Session**

School boards often handle many hot topics, disagreements, and competing agendas. To prepare for these difficult conversations, it's important to leverage the power of closed session. During this sacred time, the board will focus on questions they need clarity on so they can ask better questions in the open session. As a superintendent, utilize closed session to gauge the responses of school board members.

Although there are stiff requirements on closed session processes, many district leaders feel they can let their guard down a little more during closed session. Feel free to ask questions. Ask what you really want to ask, even if it's intimidating. Depending on the district, the closed session may be a time to vent or ask questions. Or you may need to stick closely to the closed session agenda items.

Either way, it's time to build cohesiveness and camaraderie. Utilize this time to get to know each other and get on the same page. Use this opportunity to discuss suspensions, expulsions, personnel, dismissals, and express concerns about certain people. Find out how certain board members feel about things.

It's important to build partnerships with those we disagree with by taking the time to understand their agenda and what motivates their passion. Through this relationship-building process with people who seem to make our lives miserable, many times we can find common ground and work together for the improvement and betterment of our organization. When handled effectively, this normal push and pull will create the "lift" beneath the wings of your organization and will launch you toward the skies.

## AIR TRAFFIC CONTROL

In an ideal world, superintendents, unions, and boards would work together with cohesion and mutual support. But that is not always the case. Individual board members and union members have individual requests and priorities. These competing agendas can be difficult to navigate for the top-level administrators. In times of push-and-pull, remember:

- Partner with union representation and school board members rather than cultivating an "us vs. them" mentality.
- Build relationships in advance, treating your union members and board members as fellow human beings.
- Listen and learn, using good conflict-resolution strategies and listening habits.
- Work with conflicting groups together so they can collaborate in healthy ways.

## NOTES

1. Charlie Page, "How the Atmosphere and Winds Affect Your Flight," June 23, 2019. Accessed December 15, 2022, https://thepointsguy.com/news/how-atmosphere-winds-affect-your-flight/.

2. Charlie Page, "A Passenger's Guide to Turbulence," May 4, 2019. Accessed December 15, 2022, https://thepointsguy.com/guide/pax-guide-to-turbulence/.

3. Superintendent #3, in discussion with the author, November 16, 2022. Name changed for privacy.

4. Retired superintendent #2, in discussion with the author, October 27, 2022. Name changed for privacy.

5. Principal, in discussion with the author, October 18, 2022. Name changed for privacy.

*Part 3*

# VICTORY AFTER DISASTER

*Chapter 7*

# Scanning the Horizon

*Recognizing Early Warning Signs*

There's a warning light flashing on the plane's dashboard. The radar indicates a storm is approaching. The pilot notices a wall of foreboding clouds forming on the horizon, and the warning system indicates a dangerous wind shear ahead.[1] The pilot senses a shift in the atmosphere. The wind is picking up. This is no longer the normal push and pull of air currents. This is a dangerous storm. The pilot must decide how to proceed.

Even in good weather, an experienced pilot never stops scanning the horizon for safe spots to land in case of an emergency.[2] The pilot never wants to be too far away from a cornfield, airstrip, or another safe place to land in case of an emergency. He or she is always aware of upcoming escape routes if danger would present itself.

In the same way, a leader must be constantly looking for potential hazards and ways to redirect the organization in case of an upcoming danger. The leader must always be aware of escape strategies that can be used proactively. We cannot be reactionary to things that are thrown at us. We must be in prevention mode. We can't just wait for a disaster to happen and then say, "Ok, now what?" We have to constantly prepare each day for the next.

The pandemic years have taught us the importance of detecting danger early. In 2020, some leaders were observant of shutdowns happening in other countries and started to modulate immediately. They strategized, prepared, recalibrated, and showed extra compassion and care. But other leaders crashed and burned from the constant high levels of stress during that time. All of a sudden, retirement was a desirable option for leaders who had been on the fence about when to bow out pre-pandemic. The pandemic taught us the importance of always being in prediction mode, even when disasters cannot be predicted.

As you prepare for a potential disaster, learn from the mistakes or successes of other districts or companies. When you hear about another organization going through a crisis, ask yourself: "Is our organization on stable enough footing to withstand a problem like that?"

Maybe you are so entrenched in your daily job that you never look past the current minute or hour. You are spread so thin that you never look into the future. It's critical that you start thinking about potential problems so you can get your employees cross-trained and confident. In this way, you will already have a plan in place when you have to shift and pivot.

The cockpit warning system helps alert pilots to upcoming danger. Blue lights indicate normal operations and that systems are turned on, amber-colored lights bring awareness to problems that demand heightened intervention, and red lights alert the crew to an emergency that demands immediate action.[3]

In the same way, forward-thinking leaders will choose different actions based on the severity of the problem they see on the horizon. Sometimes, the required changes may be minor—like providing more empathy to stakeholders, changing your mindset, or tuning in to people's needs. Or they could involve intentionally reshaping public perception before it takes control of the narrative. And there are times you may need to take more drastic action. The key is to notice the upcoming problems and make wise decisions about them *before* they happen, rather than reacting *after* they happen.

## BLUE LIGHT: PROACTIVE AND EVERYDAY STRATEGIES

Just like a pilot can often solve potential problems through a slight adjustment to the throttle, wing flaps, or angle of flight, a leader can often solve problems through slight recalculations. Stormy times can be an opportunity for progress and adjustments. Rather than being low points, these times can actually be opportunities to make adjustments, rebrand, and take new action to achieve realistic goals. Small problems are opportunities to prepare for larger problems down the pipe. Here are some skills that will help you make those small adjustments.

### Be Aware

First, it's critically important to keep all fingers on the pulse of the organization and the local and global community so you can start making necessary adjustments right away. You must keep tabs on the ups and downs of your people. You need to know exactly where their mindset is and have a strong understanding of organization morale. This way, you can start adjusting immediately when the disaster signs are small instead of reacting after the crash. If you notice morale problems when they are small, you might be able to make adjustments and stay in the air.

## Listen

How do you keep your finger on the organizational pulse? How will you know if morale needs to be increased? You listen. You create opportunities for people to come together and talk. You find out what people are thinking and feeling. The only way to know what your people need is to ask them and then listen.

During disasters, strategic listening is critically important. Listening is its own language in itself. Whether it's a widespread medical disaster such as the COVID pandemic or a natural disaster, children can struggle to learn during this time. Parents struggle to teach their children at home. Educators struggle with teaching on a screen. In any stressful situation, wise leaders know the best way to detect problems before they explode: listening.

The best leaders show up and listen to their stakeholders. They start weekly Zoom meetings with their families to give them an opportunity to vent and share their needs. This is tremendously impactful to stakeholders. Even if the leader can't change the parents' and teachers' tough realities, the leader's listening ear calms stakeholders and prevents angry feelings.

Listening not only benefits stakeholders but also benefits you as a leader. It gives you invaluable information about potential problems that are brewing. It will help you make decisions and develop crisis plans that truly meet the needs of staff, students, and families.

## Invite Input

While you listen, show humility. It's important to give your stakeholders a chance to share their opinions in a safe place to prevent problems from escalating. Effective communication requires humility and courage. The only way to solve complex problems is to bring together everyone who is knowledgeable about an issue, give them a place to talk, and hear them out. Be humble enough to say, "I don't know everything about this." Invite others in and truly listen.[4]

We can listen to people with different viewpoints, even if we don't agree with them at first. They can provide a valuable perspective. Tell them, "I need to stay in touch with you because I need to have the continuing perspective that you can offer to this great team."[5] In other words, be humble enough to learn from those who raise concerns.

## Communicate

A key to avoiding disaster is overcommunication. During stormy times, people in your community need accurate, timely information. During a turbulent flight, passengers often wait anxiously for an update from the cockpit. Passengers never say, "The pilot communicates with the passengers too much."

Similarly, you need to flood your people with communication. People feel unsupported when they're asking questions and not getting answers. If two months have gone by and they haven't heard from the leader, they get antsy. So send emails often if you need to. Even if you don't have all the answers, be honest about what you do know. "I don't have the answers, but I will get you the answers when I have them."

As leaders, we're not going to know everything; we just don't have enough headspace. But the good news is that it's been proven that people will gravitate toward leaders who are clear and concise about the facts they *do* have.

## Be Flexible

A key to preventing disaster is flexibility. Bryson, the military commander that you met in Chapter 1, explains that soldiers must face complex environments that challenge every fiber of their being. During warfare, they must stay flexible because these dynamic situations change faster than they can understand them.[6]

When a complex situation starts, the leader makes their best guess about how to solve it. But their first idea will often need to be tweaked for true success. That's why it's so important to make solutions adaptive. Know that you're going to have to adjust them over time.

"Our world is constantly changing," says Bryson.

> In a sports game like soccer, the rules are predictable. If you know the number of players and the rules and the environment, you can win; you can get the ball in the net. But that's not the type of situation we're facing in the twenty-first century.

With the environment changing, people making up new rules, and new players coming in and out all the time, you've got to be flexible and be ready to compete. When you see a problem coming down the pipe, you may need to make adjustments to your own level of adaptability. Become more flexible.

Learn resilience. Be a lifelong learner. In a complex environment, you may only have time to make one good move before the situation changes for you again. Keep flexing. Stay the tide.

## Let Go of Perfection

For years, Bryson focused on perfect wins during combat. But after much experience in battle, he realized this focus was shortsighted. "You don't have to win everything," he says. "You won't always make perfect decisions. Trying to be perfect is a fool's errand. What you have to do is compete very well in a complex environment."

Staying focused is more important than winning. Aim for sustained, long-term engagement, not short-term success. If you can't stay in the fight after you win once, that win is not worth very much.

## Recalibrate after Mistakes

When you are going through a bumpy situation, you will make mistakes on a daily or weekly basis, especially at first. Simply look at this as an opportunity to say, "Next time, I'm going to . . ." Be reflective, so you can truly learn something from each of those stepping stones along the way.

Don't get distracted by mistakes; we're all going to make them. Simply learn from the mistake, count it as part of the cost of boots-on-the-ground learning, and move on. No seminar or book can prepare you to be a good leader like experience can. Learning from your failures is just part of the curriculum. So when you feel like you did the wrong thing or said the wrong thing, don't waste time overthinking it.

Find a mentor to help you process your mistakes. This is critical, ground zero. Talk about your missteps with someone more experienced than you are over your favorite beverage. Let's be honest: when there's a major mistake, talking may not relieve the pain altogether, but a strong drink and a favorite friend can really take the edge off. A mentor can listen to you vent, give you some guidance, and help you feel better. Do this as many times as you need to. Always reflect, recalibrate, and get ready for the next danger.

## Mindset

What is your mindset when going through difficult situations? Do you perceive the crisis as horrible? Or do you say,

> This is freaking crazy, but it's also amazing that I've been given this opportunity to lead my staff and families through this crazy time. Not everyone has the

opportunity to be in that position. Every day, I've been given this amazing gift to influence and impact the community in this way.

It all boils down to mindset. When a warning bell goes off in the cockpit of your life, the first thing you may need to adjust is your own perspective.

## AMBER LIGHT: WINDS OF CHANGE

Sometimes, only slight calibrations are necessary to avoid danger. These include mindset shifts, communication, listening, and empathy. But other times, a natural disaster, worldwide event, or faulty community perception will demand more urgent attention.

### Building Systems for Success

Natural disasters are excellent case studies for preparing for times of crisis. Take, for example, flooding, hurricanes, pandemics, and fires; many school and district leaders have experienced them. During these times, leaders have to make major shifts and do so very quickly. Leaders had to be very good at implementing and monitoring new systems from start to finish in order to streamline the transition to safety.

Leaders are accustomed to implementing new systems; they do it all the time. But during a crisis, leaders must do so at an unusually quick pace. What made the pandemic exceptionally difficult was that most leaders had very little prep time. Almost overnight, they had to pivot from in-person learning to online or hybrid learning, a daunting task that caused overwhelming stress. The same is true of any natural disaster. It can send even the best leaders into a tailspin.

In essence, implementing a system during a crisis uses the same process as during calm times. First, bring your people together to discuss. Second, develop a plan. Next, communicate the plan to all stakeholders and partners. Finally, implement the plan and modify it as necessary.

The only difference between normal system implementation and emergency system implementation is that your time is truncated. Instead of months or a year to implement something new, you may have to roll it out in a matter of twenty-four or forty-eight hours, as was the case in the pandemic. Gaining experience in system-building can help you prepare for a crisis.

### Managing Public Perception

A pilot is not at the mercy of the winds. Even in high-wind situations, the pilot must foresee the danger, take control at any moment, and head the plane in the direction he or she decides. In the same way, leaders are not at the mercy of different agendas. We must take control of the narrative that is being published about us before it gets out of control. Perception is everything. People's truth becomes reality. In the first book of this series, an entire chapter was devoted to "Public Perception Is Everything" for exactly this reason.

A key part of detecting potential dangers is becoming aware of public narratives and perceptions about you and your organization. As a leader, you must be constantly on the lookout for dangers around perceptions. Be ready at a moment's notice to intervene. Be aware of the ways public perception may need to be modified.

As a leader, you must be the author of your own story. Otherwise, people will write your story for you. If you are not communicating a clear and consistent narrative with your stakeholders, someone will make up a narrative for you. They'll get their information from other sources, like mainstream media, their neighbor, their friends, grandma, or dad. It's your job to make sure they hear it straight from the source.

Your behaviors and decisions will be under a microscope, so make sure they are impeccable. Ask yourself, "If my actions were on the front page of the newspaper, what would that headline read?" Be very careful about social media and what you're putting out there. It can be a deadly spider web: someone will share the news with some one else who will share with someone else. And before you know it, a parent at your school is informed of your personal information and created a new brand for you. To avoid this, try to see your behavior and actions from someone else's lens.

As a top leader, public perception becomes even more important because everyone can see your every move. It's sometimes tough to handle the spotlight. But at its core, the spotlight of being in top leadership is similar to the spotlight of being a teacher. When you started as a teacher, you became comfortable with a certain degree of spotlight. Even at the boots-on-the-ground level, you were always being watched by students and families. As a top leader, it's the same concept, just on a bigger scale. You must keep the same mindset you had as a teacher: People are watching, and I need to be very mindful of the perception that people have.

Here are a few practical ways you can keep ahead of the perceptions people form about you.

## Perception of the School Board

A superintendent must stay in front of the school board's perceptions, constantly messaging and flooding information to the board. This constant communication helps the board see that good work is being done. When they're flooded with the progress of the district and know what's going on, they gain a positive perception. Even if they don't agree 100 percent with what's happening in the district or in their kids' schools, they at least know about the positives. Remember that you must constantly and consistently keep your board informed in order to shape their perception.[7]

## Communication with Staff

It's important to communicate with the staff so they don't write their own narrative about your leadership. Whenever a last-minute decision is made regarding an emergency situation, it's important to let everyone know about it, especially if it's happening on the big stage.

In one school in which a student had passed away, the superintendent emailed the entire district staff to let them know, "At this public event, green ribbons are going to be worn." The superintendent had given his okay to let this happen, but he also wanted to let everyone know about it. He didn't want people to show up to the event and wonder, "What's going on, and how come we don't know about it?"[8]

Whenever the superintendent has to make a last-minute decision, he lets his staff and board members know:

> Hey, this last-minute decision was made. I made it the best I could. If you by chance happen to be not in favor, please let me know. But I want you to be aware that tomorrow night you'll be seeing kids do such and such.

This messaging helps people stay in the loop so they don't form perceptions that get out of hand.[9]

## Perception of the Community

Communities create their own realities of the organization based on their perception of the leader. One school principal shared that her superintendent trained her to let him know immediately if something gossip-worthy takes place.[10] For example, on one occasion, a sheriff stopped in at the school and said, "Hey, you're in my area of supervision, so I thought I'd check in." As soon as the sheriff left, the principal called the superintendent instantly, just as he had trained her to do.

This wise superintendent knows how fast the rumors will start to fly. People will say, "There's a sheriff at the school. Why's a sheriff at the school?" People will start to call the district office and say, "I saw a sheriff at the school. What's going on?" The superintendent doesn't want to have to reply, "I don't know." That's why he's trained his principals to proactively let him know as soon as something like this happens. He wants to stay ahead of the messaging.

The principal needs to stay informed because he knows the word will spread. He, as the leader, needs to know what is going on. He knows he'll get school board calls that fast. Superintendents have to train their principles: "You let me know of any kind of emergency situation." Like a pilot, you must be constantly scanning the horizon, ready to change the narrative.

## Know When to Change Course

Sometimes, the solution to a possible crisis is to change the perception. Other times, the solution is to change your direction. There are times when a pilot has to completely turn the plane around or change their route to avoid a storm system or other danger that he or she sees on the horizon.

In the same way, leaders must think quickly to change course when they see an upcoming hazard. During the pandemic, some leaders and business owners saw unprecedented change on the horizon yet forged straight ahead into the storm, not thinking about strategic adjustments that needed to be made for long-term survival. Their businesses caved; we call them COVID Casualties.

But other leaders began to think quickly about how to rebrand themselves. They got wildly creative and dreamed of ways to offer services they'd never offered before. They changed gears, changed the public's perception of their organization, and showed that their company could survive and thrive, even during the constant changes of the pandemic. In short, these leaders demonstrated outstanding leadership and resilience.

For instance, Banzai International, which used to offer only in-person events, realized they had to think quickly when large gatherings were shut down. Lacking infrastructure for going virtual, they quickly acquired a Houston company that could help. Rebranding as Banzai Virtual, they rewrote their own story before the rapidly changing winds of time were able to change it for them.

Rather than accepting the narrative that they were outdated, they quickly recalibrated and built public perception. People realized, "Oh, they still offer a quality service." As a result, Banzai's recent success has surpassed its pre-pandemic bookings.[11]

Similarly, several restaurants transitioned quickly to outdoor dining during the pandemic. Catalina Island, twenty-six miles across the sea from southern California, is a perfect example of this. Pre-pandemic, only a few restaurants offered outdoor dining by the ocean. Post-pandemic, you will see beachfront dining as popular as ever. Not because the restaurant is still forced into outdoor dining due to health measures, but because the pandemic forced restaurant owners to get creative. What is better, after all, than dining with the sand between your toes and the sound of ocean breakers a few feet away?

# RED LIGHT: KNOW WHEN TO GET OUT

When the pilot hears a noise in the engine that doesn't sound good, sees a storm cloud brooding on the horizon, or notices a warning light, he or she immediately goes on high alert. The pilot must decide the relative danger of the crisis.

If the pilot suspects a severe crisis, he or she must take preventative action. Before the engine actually fails and before the storm brings dangerous conditions to the flight, the pilot may decide to find the nearest airport and land the plane. There, the mechanics can take a look at the problem, or the passengers can wait out the storm's fury. This is called a precautionary landing. The pilot lands the plane before something goes wrong. He or she knows that if they wait longer, the disaster might get out of control.

The same thing can happen in leadership. While it's important to be resilient and learn to survive the storms, it's also important to be discerning about when it is time to leave your position. If you stay too long, you may realize too late that people are sick of you. You may think, "I should have gone earlier." If you think it may be time to get out, you must quickly and decisively make the decision to cut your losses and leave before things get worse.

Gerald had been highly involved in his district for nineteen years in a variety of roles: special education teacher, high school assistant principal, special education director, middle school principal, business manager, elementary principal of outlying schools, and superintendent. You name the position; he had it.[12] Gerald moved into the role of superintendent almost by default. The person the board had in mind for the spot failed to get the appropriate certification, so the board called up Gerald in August and said, "Hey, you want to do this?"

"Sure," he agreed.

But when he took over as the superintendent in that district, he instantly had an enemy, the local billionaire. That person ran for the school board for the sole purpose of getting rid of him. When the man realized he couldn't get rid of Gerald alone—he didn't have as much power as he thought he had—he successfully stacked the board with two of his employees. The local billionaire controlled his puppet men not only at work but at the board table as well.

His puppets on the board did all the dirty work for him. For years, they fought Gerald. Eventually, things got so bad that the rest of the board members gave Gerald a vote of no-confidence. The school attorney sent a letter that said, "All the other board members voted for censure."

Humiliating newspaper articles started coming out. A half-page ad in a small-town newspaper said, "School Board Votes to Censure." Another said,

"Questions for the School District by School Board Candidate." They were questioning the hiring process by which Gerald ended up in the seat of the superintendent. There was a conflict of interest, they claimed.

Gerald wasn't prepared for the public humiliation.

"I gotta get out of here," he thought.

He realized that he had spent the past three years anxiously watching over his shoulder, unable to even sleep at night. He'd been a solid superintendent, serving on the library board and chamber of commerce, attending every basketball game, demonstrating fiscal responsibility, and ensuring improvement in student achievement.

But none of this mattered when push came to shove.

"I had to leave while I was still ahead," he said, "before I was fired."

Gerald didn't give up completely on education; he just knew that he needed to take himself elsewhere and give another district a chance. Gerald began watching school districts that were hiring superintendents. The day after the fateful board meeting, he already had an interview scheduled.

After the board meeting on Monday, he sent the paperwork on Tuesday, interviewed on Thursday, and got a job offer on Friday. Boom, boom, boom. At his new position, Gerald had five remarkable years. He realized that his first experience as superintendent did not dictate future experiences to make a difference. He also realized that most school board members in other districts have good motives and want to make his job a success.

This success came because Gerald got out in time. He moved on to the next opportunity before the school board had the chance to rewrite the narrative about him. Gerald said, "Any successful leader is just a couple of elections away from unemployment." Even if a superintendent is excellent and their students have amazing outcomes, if elected board members have ulterior motives or core values that don't align with their perception of the superintendent, the superintendent can be publicly humiliated.

At that point, is there anything that a superintendent can do to save themselves?

Gerald's advice would be, "Get your resume lined up and get out of there before they fire you. You don't want to have that on your record that you were not renewed. Keep your key in your hands and your resume warm." In other words, write your own story before someone else writes your story for you. If you feel you need to get out before they kick you out, find a way to elevate your career elsewhere or to retire.

In higher-level leadership, it's critical to develop wisdom. Be aware of upcoming problems and discern the level of danger they present. Know when it's the right time to listen and learn, when it's the right time to creatively change course, and when it's the right time to move on to a different position.

## AIR TRAFFIC CONTROL

As a leader, it's your job to scan your horizon for potential dangers and mentally prepare for them. Leaders have to be forward thinkers and big-picture problem solvers. Rather than just reacting to problems as they happen, leaders must constantly be in the mode of predicting when problems are going to occur.

- Keep in touch with the organization and understand what's going on. Listen to your stakeholders and know their concerns.
- Notice danger before it becomes a big issue. Make small adjustments in your mindset and approach.
- Stay ahead of public perceptions. Write your story before someone else writes it.
- There are times when you may need to make a big change. You may need to chart a different course or make an emergency landing. Wisdom is the key to knowing the difference.

## NOTES

1. "Airborne Wind Shear Warning Systems," *Skybrary*. Accessed March 7, 2023, https://skybrary.aero/articles/airborne-wind-shear-warning-systems.
2. "How Much of a Pilot's Training Is Emergency Landing Practices?," last modified March 20, 2017. Accessed November 30, 2022, https://slate.com/human-interest/2017/03/how-much-of-a-pilots-training-is-emergency-landing-practices.html.
3. "Warning Systems," *The Boeing 737 Technical Site*. Accessed March 7, 2023, http://www.b737.org.uk/warningsystems.htm.
4. Retired colonel, in discussion with the author, August 12, 2022. Name changed for privacy.
5. Retired colonel, in discussion with the author.
6. Retired colonel, in discussion with the author.
7. Principal, in discussion with the author, October 18, 2022.
8. Principal, in discussion with the author.
9. Principal, in discussion with the author.
10. Principal, in discussion with the author.
11. Matthieu Manzoni and Lucy Luo, "4 Innovative Business Pivots in the Age of the Pandemic," December 17, 2020. Accessed December 20, 2022, https://www.strategyzer.com/blog/4-innovative-business-pivots-in-the-age-of-the-pandemic.
12. Superintendent #3, in discussion with the author, November 16, 2022. Name changed for privacy.

## Chapter 8

# Emergency Landing

## *Character Under Fire*

Flight experts agree it's fairly simple to learn to keep an airplane flying straight. Pilots will even take children into the air, give them the controls, and let them fly for a few minutes. But the challenging part comes when something goes wrong. That's why flight instructors spend about 75 percent of their training on practicing emergency landings.[1] As licensed pilot Stan Greenspan said, "Flying lessons are not so much about flying but about emergencies. You can't 'pull over' and deal with something on a cloud someplace. You need to be aware at all times of someplace to put the plane down if you really need to."[2]

That's why it's so important to spend extra time preparing for emergency landings. A pilot who has skimped on emergency practice time will not be equipped for danger. They may be able to fake it while things are going well, but when disaster strikes, their true colors will show.

In the same way, there are many basic skills of leadership that seem easy from the outside. But when something goes wrong—which it always does in top leadership—that's when your skills are put to the test. That's when it's critically important to be prepared. A key part of top leadership is practicing character skills before the crash.

If your leadership skills were poor before the crash, they will only be magnified tenfold during a disaster. Brian Miller, a principal and site leader in Montana, says that difficulty, stress, and chaos are like a box of matches that put your character to the test. Your life is like a structure, and the trials will show whether your life is a flimsy tipi made of straw, or if it's a strong, fireproof building made of concrete, glass, and fire-resistant coating. When the decorations and facades of your life are stripped away, the strength of the underlying structure will become evident to all.[3]

Like all leaders, you have likely built an outward structure of leadership. You know how you want others to see you, and you portray yourself in a certain way. You put forward an exterior for the world to see. These outward aspects of leadership are like the external decoration and design of a house or building. It reflects what you want others to think of you.

But when leaders are faced with intense chaos, your character is put to the test. Whatever is fake or whatever is a façade burns up. The only thing that is left is the core of who you are. When your life is on fire, it shows whether the things you've built will stand the test.

Times of constant chaos bring out what is really inside of you. When Brian was a teacher, he used to tell his English students, "Any time you come across a character in literature or in life, you should listen to what they say. But really pay attention to conflict, because conflict is going to reveal their truth." In other words, it's not what people say that counts. It's what they do during times of disaster, stress, and conflict that shows their real character.

That's why it's crucially important to grow your character *before* the crash. Prepare the skills you'll need—the perseverance, resilience, grit, humility, sense of purpose, and strength of identity—*before* your life is splintering and flaming like pieces of an aircraft hurtling toward the ground.

## CONFLICT REVEALS THE UGLY IN LEADERS

Conflict reveals what is really inside a leader. If that leader has not practiced and prepared for the "emergency landing," that lack of preparation will come out in times of crisis. Some leaders' responses during disasters or highly stressful situations are a negative example of the way that chaos reveals character.

Everyone can be a great leader when times are good. When everything is going well, leaders often portray an outward persona of caring about their people. They like to say, "It's all about the kids." But under this façade of kindness, leaders' real motivation is to do whatever they want, knowing that no one will argue with such apparently selfless motivation. Their outer concern gives them a cover of protection that no one can challenge. They keep up a façade of care and concern that keeps them looking good as long as things are going well.

But when things get hard and leaders must make tough decisions, that's when their true character comes out. If a leader's core motivation is looking out for themselves, that reality will come out during times of stress. During a crisis, when the leader should be protecting those they lead, they are still making selfish decisions that can devastate the entire community. When everything else is stripped away, the selfishness at their core will become evident to all. People will see what they were trying to hide: that their decision-making has always been based on self.

The pandemic was one crisis that brought out what was really inside many leaders. Unfortunately for many, it revealed their selfishness and immaturity. Strong, respected leaders were suddenly transformed into a nightmare. They turned ugly and began making crazy decisions that neglected integrity and their people's best interests.

This is what happened to Brian's leaders in one school district where he served prior to the pandemic. The leaders emitted a persona of kindness and concern: "We're going to care for one another. This is what it means to be a leader. This is what it means to be a school district." But when the entire world entered the crucible of the pandemic, Brian's leaders showed what they were really made of.

The second that the pressure was turned up in their lives, their true identity was revealed. Under intense amounts of mental strain, the leaders started making decisions that were not based on what was best for the students or the school but on what was best for themselves or their relationships. Their decisions were based on self-preservation. They were cornered, and they wanted to self-protect. What was truly inside came out for all to see.

Ultimately, this is the reason that Brian ended up leaving the school district he was in and going to a different school district. The difference between the two districts was like night and day. In the new district, the leaders were experiencing the same hardship. They were still in the post-pandemic stage. But these new leaders were making decisions that were best for kids and best for the staff. The trial was the same, but results were very different. Seeing this juxtaposition really hit home for Brian—conflict reveals truth.

## CONFLICT REVEALS THE GOOD IN LEADERS

The pandemic crisis brought out the worst in some people, but it also brought out the best in other leaders. Rather than allowing the frantic chaos to dictate crazy decision-making, some leaders truly rose to the occasion. They said, "You know what? This is horrible and crazy, but this isn't going to shake my core values of really looking at it from a very focused perspective. What is best for my staff? For my parents? For my students? For the community?" They did not jump to rash decisions.

These leaders had prepared in advance. They'd made a habit of making decisions that were best for those they led. Any time their ideology and pride were challenged, they'd focus on responding with maturity. They had truly inspired change in their leaders, not allowing their pride to get in the way.

They cast their ego aside and did what was best for people regardless. Then, when the rubber hit the road, they were ready.

Brian has seen examples of leaders whose good character was revealed during conflict. In the past, Brian spent time as a teacher at an international school in China. He enjoyed the experience of living in China, but there were some inherent stressors that came from living in a foreign land and not knowing the language. He discovered that his glass of anxiety was often full to the brim.

Then came a situation that threatened to spill the entire glass. After his first year of teaching in China, his school needed to move campuses. It was a big deal because the school staff had to actually do the moving. There was so much transition as they simultaneously moved out of their school and their homes. Brian thought, "I'm already in another country, already in a new situation, and now I have to pick up my home and school and move." It was an incredibly stressful time.

During this crisis, the true character of the school's leadership was on full display. The leaders showed what it meant to create community and experience joy in the midst of tension. Even though they had to carry the boxes to the vehicles on a very hot, dry day, the leaders demonstrated the meaning of camaraderie. What could have been a nightmare became a powerful bonding experience for everyone.

A year later, the Chinese government wanted to repossess the new school building. As is common in China, the land belonged to the government and was on lease to the school. Now that a large development had grown up around the school, the local families wanted a school for their own local kids. They demanded the building, despite the fact that his school had a lease. There was a huge mess, and people began rioting outside the school building. Kids were trying to leave on buses, but the area was filled with rioters.

In this moment of heightened stress and conflict, Brian's coworkers walked into it with confidence. It's not that they enjoyed it, but they knew they could endure it. They remembered the excellent example that the leadership had set during the last crisis, and they felt confident they could get through anything together.

During times of stress, these leaders demonstrated what they were truly made of. Compassion was at their core. They worked hard to make sure their staff was cared for. Their goal was not just to produce good teachers, workers, or manufacturers. Their goal was to care for their employees as people. These stories demonstrate that when leaders care for their subordinates as people—their struggles, needs, and wants—those people will be enabled to face trouble with confidence. It will make a monumental difference in the way they handle crises.

Brian said, "We could go out and do some pretty great things because we felt safe. When we felt safe, we could make decisions, make mistakes, and know our leaders weren't going to squash us. That was a foundational moment for us." These leaders' true character came out during times of stress.

## PRACTICAL PREPARATION

We know it's important to prepare for trials in advance, just like a pilot practices over and over for emergency landings. But practically, what does that look like?

### Taking Time to Gain Experience

Take your time preparing for your position in leadership. It's tempting to rush into top leadership, but it's important to take the time you need to train and prepare for such a high-level role.

For example, you may have to spend time working in entry-level leadership positions, like assistant principal or learning director, to gain experience. Being an assistant principal means typically dealing with the brunt of student discipline, but most importantly, it's crucial preparation for bigger positions and bigger challenges. When you don't go through those experiences and learn from them, you don't have the skills you need to be a principal or superintendent. You can't skip the learning process.

Brian has seen the consequences of skipping the learning process. He knows a superintendent who jumped straight from being a school psychologist and program manager to being a superintendent. But since he lacked the needed training, the district ran him out of town in his first year. This was not because he didn't have a heart for kids and for staff, but because he didn't have the experience. He didn't know when to speak, what to say, or how to say it.

Now he's in his second superintendency, and the same thing is happening again. Why? Because he missed that natural progression from vice principal to principal, from director to assistant superintendent. In order to be prepared, you need to go through the slow process of training. You need to spend lots of time observing. It takes time to build character, and this is one area where shortcuts will not do you any good.

### Taking Time to Make Wise Decisions

Second, it's important to take your time while preparing for your response to a specific problem. Not only is it important to build your character in advance so you can be prepared for trials, but it is also important to take a time-out *during* trials to prepare the best response. You can't just rely on your past experience and go on autopilot, making decisions willy-nilly. You have to take the time to slow down and carefully contemplate the best action. In this way, you can be prepared when life is unpredictable and challenging you.

The leaders who often get into predicaments are the ones who rush into rash decisions without consultation and collaboration with the people that matter. They don't stop to think through the magnitude of their decisions and how they will impact their communities. They try to solve problems instantly, making grandiose decisions that match their gargantuan problems. But quick decisions are often based on personal vendettas or personal needs. When the dust settles, people can't look each other in the eye. There are fractured relationships. This type of decision-making is flawed, foolish, and unwise.

On the other hand, wise leaders take their time. It might be frustrating for their subordinates who are waiting for answers to seemingly urgent questions. But in the end, it becomes evident that these leaders are wise to put more time and thought into the decision-making process. They are strategically looking at the big picture. They ask, "How will this affect the people I lead?"

In the midst of chaos, panic doesn't help anything. It's better to search slowly for solutions. Wendell Berry, a legendary novelist and poet, said that quick solutions rarely solve the problem. In moments of panic and dramatic problems, our first urge is to find quick solutions. We want to match a dramatic problem with an equally dramatic solution. We want to solve it instantly. But that never happens. What solves the problem is a slow and methodical decision-making process based on integrity and truth.

Just like real-life injuries require time to heal, real-life problems require time to find a solution. Slow decisions set you up for real change. They give you the endurance you need to get through the dark woods of trouble. They show you the glimmer of light at the edge of the woods, but they also acknowledge that you still have a long way to go.

## AIR TRAFFIC CONTROL

In top leadership, crashes are inevitable, so you must be prepared. Build your character in advance so you can navigate the disaster with grace. Just like pilots are trained with safety measures to make sure they save as many lives as possible during a crash, you can build your character so that in the inevitable disaster, you can emerge resilient and triumphant.

- Emphasize character. Remember that a disaster will reveal who you really are on the inside. Spend time building the infrastructure of your life, not the outward decorations.
- Gain experience. Take the time to move slowly through the preparation process. Be willing to hold positions such as teacher, assistant principal, principal, assistant superintendent, and superintendent. Don't skip the training, and don't shy away from opportunities to gain experience.
- Be mentally prepared for the moment a crisis hits. Then, take your time during a crisis to prepare a helpful response. Don't rush it.

## NOTES

1. "How Much of a Pilot's Training Is Emergency Landing Practices?," last modified March 20, 2017. Accessed November 30, 2022, https://slate.com/human-interest/2017/03/how-much-of-a-pilots-training-is-emergency-landing-practices.html.

2. "How Much of a Pilot's Training Is Emergency Landing Practices?"

3. Brian Miller (principal), in discussion with the author, August 31, 2022.

*Chapter 9*

# The Crash

## *Navigating Career Setbacks*

When we see a plane crash on TV, we gasp with horror. Our eyes are riveted to the screen. The smoke, the mangled metal, and the destruction are all shocking. It's so absolutely unexpected, and we want to know all the devastating details. One of the first things we ask in this situation is, "What happened? What caused it?" We want officials to look for the flight recorder, also known as the black box, to find out what the pilots were saying before the crash. We are hungry to find out the reason for the crash.

In a similar way, a leader's termination or career rejection brings a devastating shock, not only to the leader but to the entire community. The eyes of the people are riveted to the situation. They want to know all the details. And most of all, they want to know, "What caused this?"

It's not just the community that is wondering what went wrong. When a leader experiences career rejection, he or she is the first to go into investigative mode. The leader begins to ask questions:

"What could I have done to prevent this?"
"What did I do wrong"
"what did someone else do wrong?"
"What was the reason for the rejection?"

Sometimes, this introspection and self-inspection are helpful. There are many important lessons that a leader can learn from such reflection. Mistakes and humiliating experiences can teach us lessons about areas where we need to grow in communication, skills, and wisdom. Sometimes we miscalculate a life-leadership balance, make a mistake in perspective-taking, or fail to notice and address problems while they are still small. These mistakes can lead to lessons learned and wonderful growth opportunities. We can acknowledge the part we played in these disasters and grow from our failures.

But other times, the cause of a disaster remains a mystery. No matter how hard we think, we still don't know what went wrong. We've been doing our best: admitting our mistakes, earning our staff's trust, dealing with problems before they get big, and delivering phenomenal outcomes. But we still experience times of unexpected career disappointment that can rock our world.

In air travel, there are freak accidents that take place, even when all the checks and balances are in place. And in leadership, there are career setbacks that simply don't make sense. And that's okay. At the end of the day, we may never know what the actual cause was. We may have suspected it, but we may not have been able to prevent it from happening. We may never know the precise reasons for a career crash.

Perhaps this is you right now. You are feeling so embarrassed that you don't even want to get up in the morning. You are sick and depressed and scared for your future. Just reading this now makes your heart race and your palms get sweaty. You feel embarrassed and vulnerable, which is very uncomfortable for a leader.

If this is you, know that you're not alone. The chapter on career rejection in the first book of this series, *Adjusting the Sails,* was by far the chapter that resonated the most powerfully with leaders across the globe. In other words, if you've experienced rejection, you are not the only one. By far.

Though it's a common and intensely difficult experience, it's one we don't often talk about—we need to start. When we hear other leaders' real-life stories from the field, it helps us know we're not alone. Ethan Fernandez shares his story that will surely strike a chord with many leaders.

Ethan was a model leader who led with courage, authenticity, and genuine care. As a superintendent, he had a heart for serving his community. He was passionate about making sure all children were provided with safe schools, safe communities, and safe families.[1] During his twenty-five years as an educator, he modeled authentic, honest, and humble leadership. As a result, he was beloved by his community, staff, and students.

That's why it's so surprising—and heartbreaking—that Ethan was suddenly let go of his position. Just like every leader, his life was constantly under a microscope. He was being watched and scrutinized by the public and by the community he served. To Ethan, being under the microscope had never been a bad thing. "If you are an authentic leader that upholds good character, good morals, and good values," Ethan explains, "It's okay to be under that microscope. It gives us an opportunity to be transparent, admit fault, and admit weaknesses." He was passionate, purposeful, and humble, and he had nothing to hide.

But one day, a naysayer invented a "flaw" in Ethan's life that they blew into a huge ordeal.

"When you experience the unexpected, it is a terrible feeling," Ethan says.

Even though Ethan's leadership was excellent and mature, there were people who wanted to misinterpret it. They formed misperceptions and got wrong ideas. They picked on small, microscopic areas of his life and tried to drag his reputation through the mud. And it worked.

The day after he was fired, Ethan woke up with a surreal feeling, asking himself, *Did this really happen?* After he got his bearings, he phoned a friend who had worked in education for thirty years. Over coffee, Ethan shared his pain. His friend was encouraging, and he also shared sobering words that shocked Ethan to the core.

"You know what, Ethan? Right now, no one in the community knows anything other than what is on the front page of the media. So for a while, you are unfortunately going to be considered highly toxic."

Ethan's heart fell. He hadn't realized that there was media coverage at the board meeting where he was fired. What would the news media say about him? How could he, Ethan Fernandez, be considered toxic? He had never dreamed that people would use this word to refer to him.

The next morning, Ethan's picture and a full-length story were on the front page of the newspaper. The article didn't give any details beyond "Favorite superintendent placed on paid administrative leave." But it was enough to cause deep embarrassment for this quiet, unassuming leader.

"When I saw my picture plastered on the front page of the paper, I just wanted to crawl in a hole," Ethan said. "I just wanted to pack up and leave."

The stories started to circulate. And Ethan heard them all. His close colleagues and contacts started texting him: "Did you hear that this is what people are saying?" Even though he knew that none of it was true, he cringed about the loss of his reputation. Rumors were flying. The public had perceived a false reality and they made a new truth of their own. The stories that were circulating caused him extreme humiliation and embarrassment.

The next few weeks were something that Ethan wishes no one else would ever have to experience.

"It hurt deeply to the core of my heart," he shared.

I had served in some kind of leadership in education for twenty-five years. I had gotten up every morning for 4,500 school days with a purpose and a passion in my heart. I woke up with the determination that everything I did that day was going to make a difference in the lives of other human beings, perhaps a student, a family, or a staff member that was struggling. That was who I was. That was my calling. Now, all of a sudden, I woke up and was faced with this unexpected reality.

Ethan began to doubt his value and worth. If he wasn't an educational leader, then who was Ethan Fernandez anyway? He wondered what his purpose was. It hurt so bad that he even wondered if life was worth living. "Without my educational role, who am I?" he wondered. "How can I rebuild when my life was so thoroughly destroyed? What do I do next?"

Many leaders have found themselves in similar positions: disoriented, confused, and lost. For leaders who were accustomed to the sweet success of climbing the ladder, the shock factor can be really high. After loads of success, they are all-of-a-sudden thrown into a tailspin. Because rejection is such a foreign experience, they feel intense embarrassment. They don't know how to navigate it. They need a guide, like Roni Habib.

Roni is a tremendous leader and an expert on mental health for leaders. After his own experiences of a career setback, he founded EQ Schools, an organization that focuses on enhancing the social-emotional well-being of teachers and leaders across the country. A highly engaging speaker, Roni delivers inspirational messages to thousands of people and shares deeply important insights about how to move through the pain of a career rejection.

Roni believes the healing process takes place in three stages.[2]

1. First, the initial shock. You say to yourself, "I can't believe I worked so hard, and I got such great results, yet got rejected. How could this happen?" During the first stage, you're reeling with disbelief, shock, and pain.
2. Next comes a period filled with a bunch of different emotions. Sadness, fear, and anger start to come up and swirl around in your mind. This is a confusing period of intense feelings.
3. Finally, there's the third period where you're far enough removed from the rejection that you can have a bit more perspective. You can begin to see the gifts and lessons. You begin to reflect.

Since career setbacks—and even worse, termination—are traumatic experiences all too familiar for leaders, watering down this topic is not an option.

In each one of the career rejection phases, you can gain different skills to support yourself as you move through the aftermath of the setback. First, we will explore the stage that Ethan Fernandez found himself in: disorientation and shock.

## REALIZE THE REASON FOR YOUR PAIN

To get through this first stage, Roni shares that we have to first understand the reasons we feel so devastated. Humans are neurobiologically hardwired to need to feel like we belong to an organization or group. Our brains crave connection. So when we get terminated, our brains interpret the rejection as trauma.

Being cut out of the herd and pushed away from the group is a very, very challenging and intense situation for a human to experience. Roni explains that's just how our brains work. It's the truth about *Homo sapiens*: we want to know that we belong. So when that initial shock happens, the pain is very deep.

## REACH OUT TO YOUR SUPPORT SYSTEM

During the first phase of shock, Roni recommends reaching out to your support system. If you're lucky enough to have a supportive spouse, family member, or friend in your life, you absolutely need to reach out to them. Don't forget to revisit the insights from Chapter 1 on building a strong support team. Too often, rejected leaders don't want to talk about it. It's a highly emotional subject, full of a huge amount of angst and stress. They'd rather hide. But it's so important to reach out and get support from people who will make us feel heard—people who really get us.

Relationships are the number one predictor of well-being and an important predictor of resilience, especially when we face adversity and rejection. In shock, when your nervous system is registering the pain of being kicked out of the herd, an empathetic listener will help your nervous system recognize, "I'm not alone. There is another person here with me." Even though you know it intellectually, it's vastly important for your nervous system to understand it on an emotional level. So if you have a relationship where you can be authentic and feel totally safe, reach out to that person. That's massively important.

Support also comes in the form of new faces. During a recent commercial flight from Las Vegas to Columbus, the pilot fell ill and was in great need of medical attention. The flight crew made an announcement, asking if any medical professionals were on board. Not only was a nurse on that flight to assist, but a credentialed pilot employed by a different airline was also on board as a passenger. He immediately stepped into pilot mode and helped land the flight safely.

In the same way, leaders sometimes need to let their own flight crew call for help when needed. Perhaps your immediate circle is not equipped to provide the support you need during these times of trauma, but they can put you in touch with someone who is. Instead of hushing your family and friends and swearing them to secrecy, try to be connected with someone who has been there and done that.

## REGULATE YOURSELF

After you get your support system in place, take a moment to intentionally regulate your nervous system in a specific, somatic way. When large, strong, and difficult emotions come up, we almost always sense them in our bodies. In fact, every emotion is tied to a sensation in the body.

Because our bodies are an essential but often overlooked component of our emotional health, Roni emphasizes the importance of engaging in practical, simple mindfulness practices. These embodiment practices help you notice your body and then calm yourself somatically. Take a moment to ground yourself. Sit up straight, put your hands on your lap, and check in with every part of your body. "What is going on with my jaw right now? What's going on with my heart? What's going on with my chest?" Then slow your breath down in a very intentional way. Breathe in for four counts and then breathe out for eight counts.

As you do so, your nervous system will begin to realize, "Okay, I can calm myself down somatically. I can get grounded somatically. I can get back to my head." A calm body is what keeps us present. As you calm yourself, your body will begin to recognize, "Yes, I just suffered a shock, but I'm safe. I'm feeling my body. I know I'm here. I'm breathing. I'm ok."

## SELF-COMPASSION

During the second stage of healing, you will start to have a lot of emotions surging to the surface. After the shock wears off, the confusing feelings will start to swirl in your mind. During this time, Roni shares that one of the most important skills you can learn is self-compassion. This is a very real tool that helps leaders face rejection and get through any adversity. Leaders with self-compassion can hone in and understand how to give themselves compassion in a gentle but powerful way. This enables them to move forward through adversity instead of crumbling in difficult times.

There are a lot of different techniques for self-compassion. One technique that Roni teaches is the four Ns: noticing, naming, normalizing, and nurturing.

### Noticing

When the emotions start to swirl, your job is to notice what is happening in your body. As we mentioned earlier, being aware of your body is the key to staying grounded. During this step, notice *where* you feel what's happening in your body. Is your heart racing faster as your chest constricts? Is your face flushed? Is there tension in your neck or forehead?

## Naming

Next, you need to name what you feel in your body. See if you can find words for the emotions. "I'm afraid." "I am so angry." "I am embarrassed." If you can name the emotions, you can tame them. If you try to just hold them in and resist those feelings, they are only going to persist. The feelings will only get bigger and bigger. Instead, try to put words to your feelings.

## Normalizing

After you notice your body and your emotions, it's important to normalize what you feel. Tell yourself, "Hey, I'm feeling this way because I'm human. Of course, anyone would feel this way if they were in my shoes. There's nothing wrong with me. Everybody has emotions." Hundreds of leaders get into the trap of not only having a hard time with emotions but then beating themselves up for feeling them. What's the point of that? Give yourself the permission to be human.

## Nurturing

The last step is nurturing yourself. Reassure yourself, "I am here, and I'm going to nurture and love myself." Assert to yourself, "Sweetie, I'm here for you, and I'm not leaving you. We're gonna get through this together." If you're a guy and "sweetie" is too mushy, use the word "Dude." Tell yourself, "Dude, I'm not leaving you."

With self-compassion, you will realize that you are not alone in those darkest moments. Even when things are really, really hard, you have coping skills to get through the darkness. When you realize that, you find freedom. You have full liberation. You realize nothing can stop you. You know that you're safe, and you're going to be there for yourself. You're going to be fine moving forward.

## HEALING TAKES TIME

The process of healing is not easy. Some leaders may be able to rebound in a month. For others, it might be four years. For others, it might be a lifetime. You will never forget what happened, but in order to heal, you have to learn how to forgive. It's difficult to be patient with the process.

If you break your arm, you want to find something big and dramatic that will fix your arm as quickly as possible. You want to get back to playing piano, wrestling, or playing baseball. But instead, you are consigned to ten weeks in a sling. Because that's how real problems are solved. That's how real wounds are healed: through a slow process.[3]

As leaders, we are used to being fixers and doers. When confronted with challenges or problems that are within the scope of our control, we take charge. We get right on it. We're looking for answers. We're solution-finders. We help many, many people find solutions. We like fixing things and making things better for other people.

That's what makes career setbacks difficult for leaders, as Ethan Fernandez points out. Because of the magnitude of this particular situation, there is no overnight fix. It may take several weeks or years before there's any resolution. The truth may never rise to the surface. For leaders, this is especially difficult because it's a lesson in extreme patience.

Remember Brian Miller, the leader who had to relocate his own classroom because of a leasing issue? During this chaotic time, he and his team understood the importance of the slow process of healing. While being forced to move out of their school building and homes, he and his team often took time out of the chaos to be together. They would just sit together in the same room, wallow in their frustration, and offer empathy for what was going on.

They knew that packing boxes could wait for tomorrow. Today, they just needed to find support together. This was not a fast-paced, efficient plan, but it was best for long-term growth and healing. They knew it would take time to process everything and come to a conclusion.

Frankly, when you're in the shock of a setback, the only thing you can do is take a time out, recalibrate, get support from your support system, and calm your body. After the initial shock has passed and you've gained some distance from the pain, there will be a time to move forward towards a beautiful new destination. There will be a time to look back with gratitude and take flight again in many creative ways, as we'll see in the next chapter. But for now, take care of yourself and be patient with the healing process.

## AIR TRAFFIC CONTROL

In the deep darkness of career rejection, it can feel like there's no way out. But when we realize that others have been through the same experience, it can be life-changing. Here are a few tips shared by experienced leaders.

- Remember that rejection is often unavoidable. While some failures are related to our mistakes, others simply come about as the result of others' weakness or selfishness. Even if you're doing the right work and have your heart in the right place, you may still be challenged with an unexpected setback.

- During the first stage of shock, you can reach out to your support system, calm your body, and validate your pain.
- During the second phase, when emotions start to swirl, you can notice your body, name your emotions, normalize your feelings, and nurture yourself.
- No leader is perfect, and we need to be willing to recognize our mistakes when they contribute to our rejection. But often, top leaders are rejected for reasons unrelated to their character. It can happen to anyone, despite your excellent leadership.
- If this has not happened to you but could be your reality in the future, how can you practice normalizing your emotions and noticing your body? How can you apply these principles to smaller instances of rejection in your life?
- If this has already happened to you, recognize what you have overcome. You are still standing. Remember, you are the face of resilience, tenacity, and grit.[4] Remember, you were placed in this totally unforeseen position, and yet you survived.

## NOTES

1. Retired superintendent #1, in discussion with the author, October 5, 2022. Name changed for privacy.

2. Roni Habib (executive coach, founder of EQ Schools), in discussion with the author, November 17, 2022.

3. Brian Miller (principal), in discussion with the author, August 31, 2022.

4. Retired superintendent #1, in discussion with the author, October 5, 2022. Name changed for privacy.

*Chapter 10*

# The Rubble

## *Finding Meaning in the Mayhem*

When a plane crashes, the first step is to take care of the wounded. Emergency care is provided, victims are whisked away to safety, and injuries are immediately treated.

But after initial triage has taken place, workers must revisit the crash site and start cleaning up the rubble. Plane crash sites are filled with unique risk factors: "spilled fuels, lubricants, and coolants that can contaminate soil and groundwater," as well as "biohazard or bloodborne pathogen concerns."[1]

A plane crash site needs "specialized cleaning with highly trained Field Technicians who know how to safely handle a combination hazardous materials/ biohazard site."[2] During the process of hazardous materials disposal, crews have to be careful to preserve evidence of what went wrong to hopefully determine the cause of the crash. Crews work around the clock on this specialized task.

In the same way, you will need to pay special attention to the way you clean up the crash site of your life after your career rejection. During the first step of recovery, you made it a priority to reassure your body that it was safe and that the wounded parts of your life were tended to. You grounded yourself, calmed your body, and listened to your emotions. You noticed, named, normalized, and nurtured your feelings.

Now, it's time to start picking up the pieces. It's time to revisit the smoking rubble and salvage your identity without falling into any of the hazardous and dangerous traps. It's time to reconsider, process injustice, and choose a direction for your future.

## SALVAGE YOUR CONFIDENCE

One of the first things you need to salvage from the wreckage is your confidence. Remember Carl, the high school principal who was unexpectedly fired? He was out of work for about four months. His former students showered him with love because of the investment he had poured into them over those years.[3] They boycotted and protested and almost refused to go to school the next year.

Carl had to meet with them outside the classroom and try to convince them: "No, you're going to school. This will play itself out. This will figure itself out eventually." Watching his students' passion helped rebuild Carl's confidence. He realized that he had successfully instilled passionate leadership qualities in these kids.

Another thing that helped Carl salvage his confidence was the way he dressed. "I wore dress socks every day," Carl shared. Even if he was going to work at one of the rental properties he owned, he still dressed up. "I would put on my dress socks every day because I still knew, even though injustice had happened to me, I still had to dress the part for my own mind's sake."

Carl salvaged his confidence by remembering his True North. During moments of crisis and heavy trauma, he leaned heavily on his faith. He remembered his true identity, and he expressed it in these small acts of defiant courage. "You may not see my socks all day, but they show that I know who I am, and I know what I've accomplished, and it's only a matter of time before I'm that person again."

He knew that he was not defined by his position, and losing his job did not destroy who he was as a person. At the same time, he remained confident that he had a lot to give to his profession. He would not allow one person's vendetta against him to destroy his confidence in himself and his abilities.

If you're in a similar situation, Carl urges you, "Keep your socks on, stay ready, because you'll get another opportunity again." That opportunity came for Carl when he least expected it. On a random Wednesday evening, he got a series of calls. The leader of a small town in central Mississippi wanted to get a hold of him. Carl returned the call.

> "Hey, are you interested in our superintendent position?" the leader asked him.
> Carl replied, "Sure."
> "When can you start?"
> "When do you need me?"
> "Tomorrow."
> Carl exclaimed, "Whoa!"

He told his wife, "When God calls, you answer. You have to go." He packed some clothes in the car. "Lord, you got this. Let's go."

That was October of 2017. In his new district, Carl was faced with a lot of challenges. The school district was failing and was often taken over by the state. It had a lot of good people, but just not in the right place. Carl said, "You know what? We're going to get this." He began immediately to improve the district through branding and hard work. He moved the district from the lowest of lows to the highest of highs.

## REMOVE HAZARDOUS WASTE: CONFRONT THE LIES

Remember Ethan, the gentle, much-loved leader who was fired for an absurd, tiny detail that someone pounced on? He shares additional insight that is important to recovery. Just like recovery workers remove hazardous waste from an airplane crash site, you need to do all you can to remove the hazardous waste from the community. Even though you can't change the outcome of the setback or termination decision, you can absolutely speak the truth about yourself.

Following his termination, Ethan could see how onlookers in the community were struggling to decipher who was telling the truth and how to reconcile the two sides of the story that they were hearing. On the one hand, they had their own experience, which told them that Ethan was a kind, loving, and caring leader. On the other hand, they had stories that were circulating in the media and beyond.[4]

It was difficult for Ethan to handle these lies. To a degree, he had to develop tough skin and ignore the slander. He had to remind himself at the end of every day, "God knows what the truth is, and the truth will prevail." He relied heavily on his faith and trusted that the truth would eventually come out. Ethan didn't want to get so caught up in these misconceptions that he lost touch with reality and his purpose in life. He woke up each morning and reminded himself what his purpose was. Just like Carl did, he reacquainted himself with his big why, the purpose for living that transcended a particular job or district.

At the same time, he knew he had to deal with the lies and face the deception. Like hazardous waste, these gossipers were contaminating the entire community. They were endangering his reputation. Like "energy vampires," their gossip and lies were trying to suck the life out of him and his people.[5] He knew he had to stop listening to them and not get caught up in what they were saying. But he also knew that the time had come to confront them, or the dangerous corrosion of their influence would only continue to spread.

Ethan wanted to find out where these lies and misperceptions were coming from. He decided to be bold and courageous enough to actually go out and confront the half-truths and rumors. He knew that all it can take is one lie, one cancer cell to go out and destroy an organization. There are times to be inclusive and team-oriented and to overlook offenses, but there are also times to go out and confront those people who are spreading lies. Ethan had to be that kind of leader. He had to stand up for the truth. He had to stand up and address the lies that were destroying his community.

In the end, Ethan decided to take his situation to a public trial, which lasted eight days. At the end, twelve jurors ruled in Ethan's favor. They agreed that what had taken place was not fair. Ethan thought that a twelve to zero verdict was going to change the outcome and make him feel vindicated. To a degree, it did, but he realized there was no vindication out there that would ever take away the pain and humiliation of what had happened.

The public apology he was looking for never came, but he realized that was okay. At the end of the day, he had to remember his why, and he had to accept that there will be some people who are going to believe what they want to believe, and he can't let that hold him back. Having dealt with the poisonous chemicals of lies and gossip, he had to turn toward the rubble and find the gifts hidden in the wreckage.

## SALVAGE YOUR EMPATHY

One of the gifts of career rejection is that you learn how to show more empathy towards others. Remember when Carl was falsely accused of stealing time from the district? He shares how he grew through his "crash." As he picked up the pieces of his life, he grew exponentially as a person. The trials of life brought out the strength, empathy, and purpose in him. His difficult experience of getting fired from a rewarding leadership position turned out to be the most liberating thing that ever happened to his career.

Carl's experience has given him empathy. He finds purpose in sharing his story with other leaders. He says,

> I've been where you are. In fact, I've been unemployed because of my beliefs and my standards. I want you to understand, this is not something that is lighthearted. There are moments when the whole town is against you. But we can't be 'those people.' We can't join them in their hatred and unkindness.

Because of his experiences, Carl leads from a place of understanding.

One key to healing from rejection is realizing the positive impact it has on our future and the futures of others. After you experience rejection, what are you going to do with it? What lessons are you going to impart to those around you? How are you going to use those stories and experiences to really help yourself and help others?

If you've been rejected and shared your story, other people might start opening up to you about their own career rejections. It's unfortunately quite rare for people to open up and share. No one wants to scream from the rooftops:

"I didn't get the job that the entire community thought was mine."
"I was passed up for someone I am shocked to admit got the job."
"I was terminated."

It doesn't feel like a natural topic to discuss with people. People may be embarrassed or feel judged. There are all sorts of other emotions going on for leaders who are rejected. They may think it's better to keep quiet. But if you lead the way and open up about your story, you may be opening the door for someone else to release a burden they've been carrying in silence for a very long time.

How can we help a rejected leader confide in us? And once they decide to share their story with us, how can we best support them and foster their healing? If they do find the courage to confide in us, a big trap to avoid is to try to fix it for them. It's a very common thing for leaders to want to "fix" other people's pain. But it's critical that we learn how to hold space for them without fixing their issues. Because the truth is, your job as a leader is not to fix everything. It is to empower people to fix things themselves.

## Be Present

When someone shares their painful story with you, drop everything and communicate, "You're important enough to me that I'm putting my emails aside. I'm putting my phone aside." Show them with your face that you are fully there for them. After they share, take a moment to have a little bit of silence with them. It's important when someone is sharing to be okay with silence.

Then describe to them out loud what it is that you're hearing. Just reflect back: "Wow, you've worked so hard, you've got such incredible results and yet, somehow they still did this. You feel like they don't believe in you, and I get that."

If you don't know what to say, you can just say, "I actually don't know what to say right now, and I'm just so glad you told me, because I just want to be here with you." As you empathize, you can share what this brings up for you, and you can talk about that as well.

## Get Curious about Their Experience

After listening and empathizing, there's another important piece. Tell your friend or colleague, "Hey, I noticed that this particular thing seemed really hard for you. Do you want to tell me more about it?" Be okay if they don't want to, but be open to listening if they're willing to share more. Say, "Hey, I really want to get curious with you about this."

## Avoid Taking Over

It's hard to show up for people without fixing them, but it makes a massive difference when you're trying to support someone. Usually, all the person needs is to feel seen, feel heard, and to know that this is a safe space for them to be. That will help them get through their challenges. Keep acknowledging them: "Hey, here's what I see in you." Keep reminding them, "I get that this is really hard right now. And I'm always here for you. If you need it, I'm always here for you. You're not alone." That's what people really want to know: that someone is there for them and will support them, no matter what.

Avoid the urge to jump in and lead a massive revolt to try to "save" them from the setback. A common reaction to career setbacks is to revolt against the decision. Community members may go to the school board meetings, write their emails, or gather the troops to try to dispute a decision that has been made. This almost never leads to a good outcome.

Resist your urge to "fight" for the leader. This reaction may give the rejected leader a momentary good feeling—a reassurance that you're on their side. It offers temporary comfort, like a pat on the back. But this good feeling only lasts a split second, it doesn't lead to long-term, authentic resilience and happiness. It's not actually what the rejected leader wants.

When colleagues tell a leader, "Oh, I got your back. We're gonna fight this. Here comes the revolt." They may actually be interrupting the leader's healthy healing process. Though this seems obvious and common sense, it's really a groundbreaking thought. It's critical to realize, "I'm in my power and I can support people to be in their power. I don't need to do anything beyond that."

## Provide an Example of Resilience

While you don't need to fight for a reversal of the rejection, you can help your fellow leader fight for resilience. You can pass on an example of bouncing back from trial. That's a critical point for us, especially in the twenty-first century. It's important to be wise, flexible, and balanced enough that you can pass down a legacy of resilience to the next generation of leaders. Just like one win does not define us, one loss should not devastate us. We can move forward from past disasters and stay resilient for a lifetime.

Through your own story of resilience, you can leave your mark not only on current leaders but on aspiring leaders as well. You can inspire future leaders who are looking at going into leadership positions. Let them see how you were able to work through these challenges. Show them that personal resiliency is what leaders do best. The value of any leader is measured by their ability to develop other leaders who are even more resilient than they are.

## LOOK FOR THE GIFTS IN REJECTION

Roni Habib has already shared important tips for recovering from the initial shock and pain of setbacks and rejection. He shared these personal insights from his own experience of disappointment and heartache. Earlier in his life, he was rejected as the department head in his school; he was turned down for the Design Thinking Program at Stanford that was a perfect fit for him; and he was passed over for a position at Google in their education department, even after reaching the finalist level. When he served as a teacher, a leader, and an ed tech coordinator, he experienced other experiences of being passed up.[6]

But after he got over the initial shock of being rejected from these positions, he realized that each of his experiences of rejection were actually a gift. For example, his rejection from the Stanford design program forced him to think carefully about what his heart actually wanted versus what he was expected to do. After attending Harvard for grad school, Roni had thought, "Man, wouldn't it be amazing to also do this incredible design program at Stanford and build my resume?" But after his rejection, he began to reflect on his true motives. He realized his desire was more ego-driven than heart-driven.

He began to ask himself, "Roni, what is it that you actually like? What's your heart driving you to do?" This was a gift that he found in the rubble. His rejection forced him to slow down, reflect, and direct his path toward his true dreams and goals.

After a lot of thought and connection with his heart, Roni decided to start EQ schools. Through this organization, Roni began teaching leaders to take care of themselves and become emotionally intelligent. He became an expert in helping leaders, educators, and parents become happier, more resilient, more playful, and more connected to their purpose.

Roni is sobered when he realizes that EQ schools may never have happened if he had been accepted to Stanford or accepted to work for Google. What a tragedy that would have been! Through EQ schools, he has impacted so many lives and hearts. Thousands of teachers, principals, superintendents, district and site leaders, and parents have been inspired by his message, his huge heart, and his love for people. None of this would ever have happened if it were not for his repeated rejections and disappointments.

Roni encourages you to look for the gifts that are hidden in the wreckage of your rejection. He reminds us that everything coming our way can be seen as a gift. When someone is being difficult on your staff, you can look at it as a gift for growth for yourself. When you get rejected from a position that you really wanted, you can decide, "There must be a gift here. This was meant to be. This has freed me to do what I'm really meant to do. Who knows what I was spared from, but I'm going to dedicate myself to finding the gifts in this situation."

After the initial healing process is complete, you can move on to the beautiful part of the rejection. After you have weathered the initial stages of pain and fear, you can move to a place where you can see a beautiful new destination in the horizon. Now that you're no longer tied up with your emotions like you were in the first two stages, you can shift your thoughts and your beliefs until you can see the beauty and the gifts in rejection.

You might be scratching your head right now. How can rejection be a beautiful thing? Roni's story is just one example of how rejection can lead to better roads and new opportunities.

Three Gen Z college students share their own stories of how rejection has benefitted their lives. Let's look at the gifts these future leaders have learned from their disappointment.

## Rejection Builds Perseverance

Benjamin is a Gen Z student who thought he was good enough to make the varsity team in high school sports. He had confidence in himself and believed he could go somewhere. He thought he met all the qualifications to make the team. When he was told he wasn't good enough, he had to take a step back and look for ways he could improve himself.[7]

His early rejection became fuel that helped him drastically improve himself through his senior year. His failure was a big lesson, and his story became fuel. He has realized that everyone is going to experience some level of rejection that makes them feel like they aren't good enough.

All of us will have someone tell us we aren't good enough. Failure is inevitable, and we can use it as a motivation to improve. Benjamin says:

> Rejection can be a tremendous positive, because you are able to build off of that. At the end of the day, if you fall down ten times, you get up eleven. You push through your day and you get better from it.

Benjamin is now a junior at San Jose University, a business major with a minor in economics. His goal is to continue to work on his real estate license and eventually own his own brokerage.

## Rejection Makes You Flexible

Another college student, Anya, reflected on her experience of getting multiple rejection letters from colleges. When she didn't hear back right away from some of her top schools, she started feeling discouraged. When she ended up getting rejected, she felt even worse. At the beginning, it was so hard to see the good because she felt like a failure, not accepted, and not good enough.[8]

As we all should do, Anja tried to find the light and the good in what she had. She realized that there's always good that comes out of failure and rejection. In her case, like Roni, it helped redirect her toward where she was supposed to be. Since she wasn't accepted into her preferred school, she had to look through other options. She chose the University of Arizona, an option that she wasn't 100 percent sure about. But it has been a fantastic experience that has shown her the importance of "going with the flow and seeing where things take you."

She is now a pre-business major. She is considering a management and marketing major with a minor in communications. Anya can now say honestly, "Failure is one of the best things that can happen to you, because you're able to grow and find what you're supposed to be doing through failure."

## Rejection Gives Creativity

A third student, Joseph, experienced a lot of rejection in high school. He was extremely academically oriented, and he was also trying to be a three-sport athlete. He faced a lot of hardship trying to get onto the soccer team, even though he had played for fourteen years of his life.[9] Having that early disappointment forced him to look for an alternative path, which in turn helped guide him in the direction that he is going today. He has learned to overcome the challenges and adversity that he faces, even when things look different than he expected.

Joseph is currently studying human biology at Stanford University with the hope of entering the field of Ophthalmology and going to med school. He explains that most students at the university he comes into contact with have had a prosperous academic life and didn't have a lot of competition in high school. They haven't had the chance to learn lessons from failure.

Joseph is grateful he has had the chance to fail and be humbled. He says, "Experiencing that failure pushed me to go outside the box, try something new, and look for other ways to study and approach new challenges that arise." In other words, failure made him more flexible and creative.

## Rejection Contributes to a Growth Mindset

What did you notice in all of these Gen Z students? Each one of them is comfortable talking about failure. That's due in part to the extensive influence of Carol Dweck's philosophy. The growth mindset philosophy is grounded on the fact that mistakes, failures, rejection, and bumps on the road are part of the life process. Whether academic, athletic, personal, or professional, these disappointments are part of the natural process that eventually makes our brains stronger and better at what we're doing and how we're contributing to society.

Gen Z students were exposed to Dweck's growth mindset concepts in elementary or middle school, and it has had a profound impact on them. They have clearly taken this philosophy to heart.

**Rejection Teaches You to Make the Most of Every Moment**

The last gift of rejection comes to us through the story of Carl, the principal who was fired from the high school position. Carl says his rejection taught him to make the most of every opportunity. "Everything is transient and nothing is guaranteed, so make the most of it before it's too late," Carl says. Carl has realized that nothing in his profession is guaranteed. In whatever position he occupies, he realizes he may not have this seat tomorrow. So he challenges himself: "What am I going to do with the position while I have it?"

Carl wants to make sure he leaves an impact with no regrets. He urges you to do the same: "Do it now, and if you make the right decision, you can go to bed at night knowing you did what was right."

## FIND YOUR OWN GIFTS OF REJECTION

What are the gifts of your rejection? How has your disappointment freed you from ego? How has it driven you to become more passionate and authentic? How has it helped you be more flexible, find your purpose, or make the most of every opportunity?

As you start to shift your beliefs, you begin to recognize just how big the world is. Sure, you've been rejected from this one position, but there are so many other places out there that would love to have you. There's a place for you and a time for you. Rejection can be a gift because you can find new careers and new horizons.

When you begin to experience positive emotions of gratitude about your rejection, you are now open to new possibilities. Dr. Barbara Fredrickson from the University of North Carolina found that when people elicit positive emotions through gratitude and positivity exercises, they actually become more creative. They're more collaborative, they want to learn more things, and their eyes are open to all of the possibilities—literally and figuratively.

The world is much larger than you think. There are so many opportunities ahead. And that is exactly what we will explore in the next chapter.

## AIR TRAFFIC CONTROL

If you've ever been fired or passed over for a prominent position, you know what a low point this experience truly is. Your world is spinning. Nothing can emotionally prepare you for this pain. You were doing well and had every reason to expect that you would be successfully employed for many more years. And suddenly, the carpet was ripped out from under you. In those moments of trial, here are some tips that can help you sift through the wreckage.

- Keep your confidence. Remember who you are. Take small actions that will remind you that you still have a lot to offer the world.
- Resist lies. When possible, stand up for the truth and root out the source of the myths and rumors that threaten to ruin your reputation.
- Find the gifts. Even in the wreckage, there are blessings. Keep your eyes open for those benefits.
- Give those gifts to others. Find someone else who is going through a similar situation. Offer them the gift of your story, your listening ear, and your resilience.

## NOTES

1. "Plane Crash Cleanup," *S&R Environmental*. Accessed March 10, 2023, https://www.srrenviro.com/sub-services/plane-crash-cleanup/.
2. "Plane Crash Cleanup."
3. Superintendent #2, in discussion with the author, September 1, 2022. Name changed for privacy.
4. Retired superintendent #1, in discussion with the author, October 5, 2022. Name changed for privacy.
5. "Energy vampires" is borrowed from John Gordin.
6. Roni Habib (executive coach, founder of EQ Schools), in discussion with the author, November 17, 2022.
7. Benjamin (student, San Jose State University), in discussion with the author, November 30, 2022.
8. Anya (student, University of Arizona), in discussion with the author, November 30, 2022.
9. Joseph (student, Stanford University), in discussion with the author, November 30, 2022.

*Part 4*

# JOURNEY'S END

*Chapter 11*

# Taking Flight Again
## *Discovering New Purpose*

On July 15, 1942, during World War II, "six P-38 Lightning fighter aircraft and two B-17 Flying Fortress bombers"[1] took off on their way to Iceland.[2] They were ultimately headed to England to support the Allies in their war against Hitler in World War II. But on their way, they ran into dense fog and a blizzard. The planes were running low on fuel. Unable to communicate with their safety team due to a German submarine's interception, the planes were forced into emergency "belly-landing on the ice" in Greenland.[3] "Though all the crew members were rescued nine days later, the aircraft were left behind."[4]

Fifty years after this event, a team decided to uncover and rescue one of the airplanes. Searchers thought the airplanes would be on the surface, but they were actually buried under 263 feet of ice. Thirteen attempts were made to uncover the planes. The first plane they found had been crushed by the ice and could not be salvaged. But then they discovered "Glacier Girl," a plane with stronger body armor that had withstood the pressures of the ice. They melted a tunnel to the plane, crawled down to where it was buried, pried the parts apart one by one, and pulled them back up to the surface.[5]

The recovered plane was shipped to a small town in Kentucky, where the mastermind of the project lived. He began restoring the plane, one piece at a time. His goal was to "restore the plane to the condition it was in when it left the airport."[6] It was difficult to find parts for such an old plane since only 80 percent of the original pieces could be saved. Sometimes, he had to manufacture the parts himself. He purchased a blueprint from the Smithsonian so he could fix and manufacture each new part "right up to the specs" of the original project.[7]

It took ten years to rebuild the plane. "The Lightning returned to the air in October 2002."[8] The creator's goal was to enable this lost plane to finish its flight to Iceland. "On July 22, 2007, *Glacier Girl* departed" from New Jersey "in an attempt to fly across the Atlantic Ocean to Duxford, England, to complete the flight it had begun 65 years earlier."[9]

Here is a question for you: Do you feel like that plane? Has your life been frozen for many years under layers and layers of fear, shame, disappointment, and rejection? Perhaps you continued to carry out your daily duties after your career disappointment. But on the inside, you were frozen, a shell of who you once were as a leader. For you, excavation might take a long time, and it might take restoring yourself piece by piece. But it will be 100 percent worth it. It's time to fly again.

In these previous chapters, we've hit hard on some really critical pieces that many leaders can relate to. Whether you have experienced career rejection in the past, whether this is your current reality, or whether you're anticipating that you may face it in the future, you can probably find yourself in these pages. We've seen that rejection can lead to opportunities for you to show empathy to others who are going through the same experience. It can lead to flexibility and new directions, and it can lead to new beginnings.

## FIND A NEW PURPOSE

Sometimes, rejection can lead us in a completely new direction. Remember Ethan, the beloved superintendent who was unfairly fired against the desires of his entire constituency? After the rejection, Ethan lost his sense of purpose for a while. He had thought his purpose in life was to serve children and school communities.[10] But after a time of reflection, he began to realize that he was being guided toward a new venture. Ethan decided to take a completely new path. He left education entirely and began his own business. He also became involved in nonprofit organizations.

In this new capacity of leadership, he now runs a successful business. He also stays in daily contact with the community he loves. He serves on the board of directors and as chairperson for the county child abuse prevention council.

Ethan realized that his purpose—his "why"—was still the same. He was still serving children. He could still find ways to be a bright light that would shine in others' lives, just as he had when he had served twenty-five low-income districts.

Ethan has found a new purpose in his life, and he encourages others to find similar life-saving devices. "Find the parachute. Find the life raft," he says. "When you're ejected from the plane, grab the parachute on your way out."

## FIND NEW HORIZONS

Daniel Seddiqui is another leader who decided to take a new path after experiencing over one hundred rejections. We have so much to learn from Daniel, whom *USA Today* named "The Most Rejected Man in the World." At USC, Daniel got great grades and competed in track and field and cross-country. His school had one of the best national programs in the country, so he thought his track experience would look good on his resume. With all his good attributes and skill sets, he was sure he could get an entry-level job. He was not anticipating the level of rejection that was awaiting him.[11]

After graduation, Daniel was invited to many interviews based on his resume. He was even invited back to the second and third rounds of interviews. Often, he paid his own way across the country to his interviews. Once, he flew from Chicago to Palo Alto for a third-round job as an accountant for the men's tennis team. This was his dream job; he was qualified for it, and he was very excited. But after all this expense, the organization said, "Oh, sorry, we went with another candidate."

The same scenario played out over and over in an unbelievable career horror story. Time after time, Daniel was rejected. Several times, the company's new hire quit after a few weeks or months, and the company would call Daniel back for more interviews. But then they would reject him all over again. In total, Daniel went through 120 rounds of job interviews and got zero offers.

"How could they treat me that way?" Daniel wondered. "How could they give me such a sense of being qualified and then reject me? They were giving me false hope. It was like dating when the other person leads you on and then dumps you."

Daniel still isn't sure why he didn't get hired. Perhaps it's because he had no real-world experience besides being an athlete and a student. Either way, the interviews helped him realize that he didn't actually care about the field he was attempting to go into. He was only trying to get a job in this field because he thought it was his fate. He was following his family's footsteps, the safe road, the road of familiarity and tradition. It was expected. It was his duty. But it wasn't his passion.

### Follow Your Passion

After 120 disappointments, Daniel realized he needed to pursue something that really sparked his passion. As a six-year-old kid, he had always been curious about maps. He used to stare at maps for hours, thinking, "Whoa, what would life be like if I lived in a different environment?" Now, as he tried to figure out the right career path for his life, he decided to follow his curiosity instead of the path of least resistance.

Daniel realized he was interested in learning about all the different industries that made up America, as well as the cultural aspects of different parts of the United States. So he decided to try something completely novel: getting a job in every state in the United States. Fifty jobs in fifty weeks in fifty states.

Daniel started sending out hundreds of emails. He made dozens of cold calls. In those days, it wasn't common to apply for jobs remotely, but he did all he could to connect from a distance. He would think about an industry, look them up, and find ways to contact them directly. He called corn farmers in Nebraska, zoologists in Washington, loggers in Oregon, cheese makers in Wisconsin, and coal miners in West Virginia. His heartfelt passion told him he was on the right track.

## Take Rejection in Stride

Daniel had finally discovered what was worth putting his energy into. He decided to follow his interest, even if he got a lot of rejection. He expected to hear the word "no." Because he was doing something no one had ever done before, he knew that hearing the word "no" would be part of the process. But that was not going to be part of the equation that determined whether or not he would continue to pursue his passions. "I, Daniel, am the only one who will decide when I will stop—not anyone else's 'no,'" he said. "I am the one who will decide how much rejection I am willing to take for my dream."

Daniel encourages others to take the same approach. "If it's something that's worth pursuing, you're the only one that can stop you," he shared. "The word 'no' is not going to stop you."

Three months later, Daniel got his first yes, in Nebraska. Before he hit the road, Daniel's uncle told him, "If the 'why' is strong enough, the 'how' comes easy." Daniel's "why" was very strong, and the "how" was beginning to pick up steam. At twenty-five years old, he had zero money, but he bought a Jeep with a credit card. Then he launched out to the Nebraska corn fields. Even though he didn't have a second job lined up for the end of the first week, he figured, "I can work one week in Nebraska, sleep in my car for a week, and see how that goes."

It had taken Daniel three months to find his first job, so he wondered if it would take another three weeks to find his next one. But soon the calls started coming thick and fast. Because he had laid so much groundwork and sent out so many emails in the past months, it only took him a couple of days to find another "yes." Responses started pouring in from people who had gotten an email or phone call months earlier. Daniel got five job offers within the next ten days.

So he pulled out his map and began scheming: "How am I gonna logistically go from working in Nebraska to Florida? I'm going to have to map this out." It became a puzzle, and as he put the puzzle pieces in place, he felt very excited. His new life purpose was becoming a reality.

Once Daniel had found his passion, it changed the way he viewed his rejection. He was still getting rejection emails as he attempted to find jobs in all fifty states. He sent out a total of eighteen thousand emails, and the vast majority of those were rejections. But now that he had found his passion, it made the rejection worth the pain.

Because he was pioneering a new space that he was passionate about, he didn't mind the rejection as much. He came to see it as a numbers game. He knew there were many things he couldn't control, but there was one thing he could control: his mindset and emotions. He chose to view his rejections as a gift that helped him find what he was truly passionate about.

After he started out in Nebraska, he began to line up projects in other states for other positions. He started to meet a lot of people and ended up not having to sleep in his car very often at all. He would roll into the state as a stranger, but people would hear about him and offer him a place to stay. By the time he got to the worksite, he was no longer a stranger. They asked him, "Where are you staying?" If he said he didn't have a place to stay yet, they'd say, "Come stay with me."

Daniel was literally hired for fifty jobs in fifty states in fifty weeks. Every Monday, he encountered a new job, a new state, and a new family. He worked as "a corn husker in Nebraska, a logger in Oregon, a cheese maker in Wisconsin, and a surfing instructor in Hawaii."[12] After he finished his tour, Daniel wrote a book that chronicled how he turned "rejection into opportunity, and dreams into reality."

## See Disappointment as Direction

Daniel says it's important to look at disappointment from the right perspective. He explains, "You can look at disappointment in one of two ways. One is to say, 'I'm really disheartened. It's just hard. I've lost confidence, self-esteem, energy, and money. All these tangibles and intangibles are just out the door.' Or you could say, 'Wow, thank you for that fork in the road. I'm happy where I ended up, the direction I chose, and choosing me."

If you look at it from a religious standpoint or a universal standpoint, your direction is already chosen for you. Your path is chosen, and it's up to you to figure out what that is. You're going to be in that direction regardless. So be fearless. That doesn't mean you just sit back and let life happen. Instead, it means gaining the confidence to know when to put your heart into something. Your heart will tell you how much rejection and disappointment you're willing to withstand for your dream. It will tell you to keep on trying, or it will tell you to try a new direction. And it will lead you to where you're supposed to be.

Daniel began to accept every rejection as a redirection. He believes that every experience, every path that he took, only happened because he was rejected by another. For instance, during his fifty-state tour, he was rejected by the bourbon industry. He's grateful that it happened, because that gave him an opportunity to work on the farm and deliver Thoroughbred horses for the Kentucky Derby. The alternative happened to be better.

He realizes that each opportunity he had was a direct result of rejections from other places. Each relationship he built, each memory he made, and each experience he had would not have happened if he had been accepted elsewhere. It was tough to withstand rejection, but he learned to accept the uncertainty of where life was leading. He came to see that rejection could be an open door.

## Gain Confidence

Daniel's experiences built up a shield for him to deal with rejection and disappointment, and he takes that perspective with him into the future. Because of his outlook, he gained the confidence to say, "If I want to do something, I can do it. If I want to be an athletic director for a large Division One college, I can do it. If I want to be another best-selling author, I could do it." By now, Daniel has garnered nearly eighty thousand rejected emails in the course of all his adventures. But he doesn't allow that to stop him.

Daniel clearly had stories and lessons to share, so he decided to seek out publishing options. He said to himself, "You know, I don't want to self-publish this book. Let me see if I can get a publisher." So he went to his local bookstore to get inspiration. He went to the travel section and contacted every publisher that he saw.

He got rejected by all of them. "Here we go again," he thought. But then finally, a publisher said, "Yeah, I love your concept!" The concept for his book was to break the U.S. map into ten cultural regions and create a tour for each one. His publisher loved the concept so much that they said, "We want you to make a book for each one of those tours." Daniel is excited about making a book for the Music South, nautical New England, a beverage theme in the Northwest. He plans to make ten books in all, honoring the love of maps and exploration that he's had since he was very small.

"My dream as a six-year-old kid looking at maps still exists as a forty-year-old man. I'm still involved with maps, exploration, and curiosity. Just look where the rejection led me."

## Never Stop Dreaming

"Dreams are never over," Daniel shares. After his book was published in 2011, Daniel knew he had to find something new to do. He had to continue to challenge himself and build on the things he'd started. So Daniel founded an internship business for students. He helped students gain the career insight he never had as a youth, so they would be prepared when they graduated. As he worked with one hundred universities to equip students for their career futures, he turned his own bad experiences into something that could help others.

Over the next few years, Daniel embarked on several more trips, eventually traveling the entire United States over twenty times. He sang with the Mormon Tabernacle Choir in Salt Lake City, shot archery with members of the Cherokee Nation, and built furniture with the Amish. On his fourth American journey, he crafted a piece of art in every major city in the country.

> He made graffiti art in New York City, fortune cookies in San Francisco, a model car in Detroit, a Scandinavian butter knife in Minneapolis, BBQ sauce in Kansas City, sand art in Miami, a Mardi Gras mask in New Orleans and even a tea chest to signify the Boston Tea Party in Beantown.[13]

Daniel charted his own course, fueled by a lifelong love of maps and meaningful connections. He went on to become a multi-time international best-selling author, keynote speaker, career education entrepreneur, and travel entrepreneur. His work has been featured on many mainstream media outlets, including CNN, Fox News, MSNBC, NPR, *The Today Show*, the *Wall Street Journal*, and *USA Today*.

Daniel has not only been called "The Most Rejected Man in the World," but he has also been titled by some media outlets as "The Most Traveled Person in America" and the "The Most Ambitious Job Seeker." All because he was not afraid to launch out in new directions. To him, rejection is just a way of helping your heart find its way and the passion you were meant to live for.

## THINK BIG

One of the biggest takeaways from Daniel's experiences is that it's wrong to assume our current organization is the only place in the world for us. It's easy to get stuck in a rut, but it's important to remember that there are other opportunities out there. If we're rejected from a position or, even worse, terminated unexpectedly, we feel like life is over. We feel like there's nothing left for us beyond this place.

What is incredibly refreshing is that Daniel squashes that mindset. Not only was he resilient through the process of rejection in general, but he's showing people that there is a vast world out there, full of opportunities beyond our wildest dreams.

"We're not a tree, growing where we are planted. We can change. If we don't like where we are, we can move," Daniel reminds leaders. Daniel is grateful his rejection led him beyond his little bubble in California. He got to experience diverse cultures and landscapes across the country—something he would've never done if he stayed in the small circle where he grew up.

A career rejection can be a release from a job that isn't in line with your passions, as Daniel's early job opportunities weren't.

### Why Grieve Rejection from a Job You Didn't Love?

Why are we so devastated about losing something that wasn't truly in line with our passions at all?

The rejection may actually give you permission to realize how unhappy you were. It opens the door to freedom, ushering you into the next opportunity. Like Daniel, your rejection may be telling you it's time to pursue what you actually love.

Rejection can be a blessing in disguise, helping you find the path that will bring you the most joy and the job that will add the most value to the world. Frederick Buechner has famously said that the place of your calling is "the place where your deep gladness and the world's deep hunger meet."[14] You can move forward to a new calling. Are you willing to take that next step?

## TAKE THE RISK OF NEW BEGINNINGS

When your system, your old leadership position, or your old dream must die, it's important to learn to hope again. Roni says that after the initial recovery stages after a setback or rejection, dreams may start swirling around in our minds. But when they do, those dreams can feel terrifyingly vulnerable and risky. Pursuing a dream means jumping hard and jumping high. The risk is scary.[15]

Roni reminds us of a powerful message from Albert Einstein: "The most important decision we make is whether we believe we live in a friendly or hostile universe." The answer to that question will often determine whether or not we move forward to take the risk.

As you learn to trust that there is good in store, you can take the plunge. Bryson, the retired colonel, urges,

> Please stop waiting. Holding off until it's perfect will have you holding off until you die. Then you're going to die with a heart full of dreams, a soul full of energy, and a lot of what-if regrets. Take action, create something you're proud of. And take that first step.[16]

## AIR TRAFFIC CONTROL

As you recover from career setbacks or rejection, you may find yourself considering new careers, new horizons, and new opportunities. Rebuilding your dream takes time, but it is worth it.

- Learn to tolerate rejection. Don't let anyone else's "no" determine your future. You are the only one who can decide to stop pursuing a dream and take a different path. Don't let anyone else determine that for you.
- Be willing to take the risk. Deal with fear and trust that you live in a friendly universe.
- Remember that disappointment can be a direction. A rejection in one area often means an open door in another area.
- Many times, the job you were rejected from wasn't even in line with your passions. Be willing to let go of an old career you didn't even like. It's time to embrace something new.

## NOTES

1. Jay Bennett, "WWII P-38 Discovered Under 300 Feet of Ice in Greenland," last modified July 27, 2018. Accessed February 1, 2023, https://www.popularmechanics.com/flight/a22575917/wwii-p-38-discovered-under-300-feet-of-ice-in-greenland/.
2. "World War II Planes Found in Greenland In Ice 260 Feet Deep," August 4, 1988. Accessed October 20, 2023, https://www.nytimes.com/1988/08/04/us/world-war-ii-planes-found-in-greenland-in-ice-260-feet-deep.html.
3. "World War II Planes Found in Greenland."
4. Bennett, "WWII P-38 Discovered."
5. "The Lost Squadron," PBS. Accessed February 1, 2023, https://www.myarkansaspbs.org/programs/lost_squadron.
6. "The Lost Squadron."
7. "The Lost Squadron."
8. "Glacier Girl," Wikipedia. Accessed February 1, 2023, https://en.wikipedia.org/wiki/Glacier_Girl.
9. "Glacier Girl."
10. Retired superintendent #1, in discussion with the author, October 5, 2022. Name changed for privacy.
11. Daniel Seddiqui (speaker, author), in discussion with the author, November 21, 2022.
12. Molly Given, "How Daniel Seddiqui was able to 'Piece Together America.'" Accessed December 15, 2022, https://metrophiladelphia.com/daniel-seddiqui-piece-together-america/.
13. Given, "How Daniel Seddiqui."

14. Frederick Buechner, *Wishful Thinking: A Theological ABC*. Accessed March 28, 2023, https://www.goodreads.com/work/quotes/118728.

15. Roni Habib (executive coach, founder of EQ Schools), in discussion with the author, November 17, 2022.

16. Retired colonel, in discussion with the author, August 12, 2022. Name changed for privacy.

*Chapter 12*

# The Destination
## *Sustainable Leadership*

Pierre is a pilot who loves adventure. In fact, he calls himself "The Pilot Who Explores." Before the pandemic, he traveled to thirty countries in just one year—and that didn't include the places he flew for work. COVID didn't stop him. He has traveled to seventy countries in the three years since the pandemic, despite air travel restrictions.[1] To Pierre, enjoying the destination is just as important as enjoying the journey.

But pilots can't get fixated on just one long-term destination. Instead, they enjoy every small destination along the way. Some pilots and flight attendants will make use of layovers to stand in front of the Taj Mahal, enjoy the colorful streets of Venice, or gaze at the sparkling waters off Seonyudo Beach, South Korea. The long-term destination is not the only thing that's important to them; they also take the time to enjoy the sights along the way.

The same is true of leadership. Sometimes, we get so carried away with long-term destinations—a higher position, a full retirement—that we forget to enjoy the journey. We forget to enjoy the moments of destination that are with us every day. And we forget to take time to rest and become truly reflective of where we are, where we've been, and where we're going.

Maybe you're saying to yourself, "There's no time for me to stop and enjoy the scenery. I'm not retired. I'm not done." But remember, part of reflection is being able to adjust and make changes. And you need to do that *before* you retire, not after. Even if you haven't reached your ultimate career destination, you can still take time to pause and reflect on where you are, where you've been, and where you're going.

Think of these times of reflection as pit stops. Or as a layover in an international airport. Pilots who truly love traveling find ways to pause, reflect, and relax—even during layovers along the way. At first glance, it seems impossible that you could sleep in a comfy smart bed, take a walk in a park, or go to the library during a layover. But is it really as impossible as you think?

The Amsterdam airport would prove you wrong. Everything about the airport's surroundings screams: "Take a break. Rest. Enjoy yourself. You're still not at your destination, but you can stop and reflect for a minute!" You might be surprised at what this airport offers. Inside it is an art museum, which features rotating displays of Dutch artists such as Van Gogh. There's a mini science museum for kids, which has interactive displays where kids can "make sound waves visible, tame electricity and blend [their] face with someone else's."[2]

The airport offers a shopping mall, sixty restaurants, and a library where people can borrow books or leave behind books they've finished on the trip. There's a gym to work out, sleep pods to rest, three playgrounds for kids, and parks with real trees.[3] Finally, there is a meditation room for rest and relaxation. Interfaith church services are held for travelers who missed their religious services while traveling. Airport chaplains are available around the clock to help travelers with crises and "emotional problems surrounding your departure or arrival at the airport."[4]

You wouldn't have thought that an airport layover could be an oasis that would leave you relaxed and refreshed.

And the same is true for your life. You don't think you have time to stop and reflect, but think again. Open your eyes to the beauty and opportunity all around you. Take the time you need to refresh yourself, to walk in a park, to stop and meditate—even if it's just in the brief layovers between life emergencies.

There's no reason why you can't take time out to reflect on your journey—even if you feel like you only have a three-hour layover between yesterday's crisis and tomorrow's.

Consider this a pit stop.

The leaders in this chapter are going to give you a few extra perks to help you put your feet up and ponder your life and your future. Can you take a moment out to reflect on your journey so far, to think about the future, and to recalculate?

One day, you'll be able to join those retired leaders you envy. You'll be able to plop down and wiggle your toes in the sand with your favorite beverage in hand. You'll be able to decompress and let yourself enjoy the much-anticipated moment. But for now, you'll need to enjoy the pit stops and learn from the joys, sorrows, mistakes, and triumphs of seasoned leaders.

Every stop along the way is a destination of some sort. Yes, there will be other flights ahead. But it's important to take time to rest and recharge. Let's listen to some lessons from leaders who have reached their final destination and are reflecting on their journey. As you read these educators' insights, take a moment to rest, decompress, and reflect on where you've been and where you're going next.

## REFLECTIONS ON ACCOMPLISHMENTS

Renée and Diane, retired administrators, are pondering their lives, and they encourage you to do the same. Renée retired as a superintendent and Diane as a deputy superintendent in the same district. Together, they share fifty-plus years of leadership experience. Renée and Diane will share some of the things they are most proud of, the mistakes they made, and the trust and respect they built in their community.

### Equipping Staff

Renée and Diane are proud of the culture of respect they built through equipping teachers, allowing freedom, and building interpersonal skills. They are most proud of being part of an organization that built capacity in staff. Whether that staff was a bus driver or a teacher, Renée and Diane focused on building up their employees. They realized that the best gift they, as leaders, could give was the investment they made in their people. They constantly asked themselves, "How can I leave an impact on the people in my care? How can I make their lives better?"

Diane agrees that one of their most important areas of impact was how they equipped and empowered teachers. They taught teachers to not only teach standards but also keep their own unique approaches to education. They successfully shored up areas where teachers needed improvement. They built capacity in teachers and kept accountability for everyone in the organization. They also worked hard to make sure their principals were equipped and supported so they could in turn support teachers. They realized that the superintendent's knowledge was irrelevant if the principal wasn't capable of leading change.

### Culture of Respect and Care

Before she was superintendent, when Renée was a teacher, she began to realize the importance of a positive building culture. As a teacher, she could instantly sense the culture in each building she entered. When she later became a superintendent, she learned to emphasize culture, values, capacity, and social-emotional skills.[5]

Diane agrees that culture and respect are always important. They placed an emphasis on interpersonal relationships, which are so important to a positive culture. They built trust and mutual respect. They knew that, in order to be true and authentic leaders, respect must come first.[6] They both recognized that if they lost someone's respect, it was very difficult to win it back.

Diane sought to build a culture of care, even when delivering difficult news to staff members. At one of the schools she worked at, there was a very sweet teacher who was nonetheless a very poor match for the school. Diane sat in on her class and realized, "This is a mistake. She is not good for the kids." Diane began spending time with the teacher and talking with her about her teaching and her position.

Diane is very proud that the teacher felt respected throughout the entire process. The teacher eventually realized that education was not a good fit for her. She later came back to Diane and brought flowers and thanked her for her kindness: "I can't tell you how much I appreciate you coming and sitting down with me and talking with me and helping me see that I needed to do something different."

Another time, one high school teacher knew his content but was mediocre as a teacher. After the debrief, he said, "You don't know how good you made me feel." She had just given him some things to work on, yet he said, "You are the first person in twenty-five years who has ever given me anything corrective. You did it in a way that I feel good about myself." The culture of understanding and respect that Renée and Diane were creating made a huge difference for these staff members.

Furthermore, Renée and Diane tried to be understanding when the teachers were exhausted. Even though the top leaders had research to back up their actions, they were also sensitive to the teachers' needs. They wanted to be aware of how the implementation was actually going. They were open to the possibility that the teachers were on overload and they needed to slow down. These approaches built trust and a positive culture.

## Wise Hiring and Firing

Renée and Diane placed an emphasis on hiring the right people. They put a lot of work into finding the best staff. They sat in on every interview. They required that each teacher give an in-person lesson in front of live children. They knew the most important thing was not what a teacher knew, but how well they could teach. When they saw teachers in action, they would realize which ones had a natural demeanor with children and which ones didn't. That requirement showed how serious they were in their intent to offer the best for the children.

Renée shared that they were not only careful when hiring, but they were also supportive of teachers who were not doing well. If someone was on a plan of assistance for two years in a row, that person received a lot of support. Teachers who didn't like their evaluation could ask for another evaluator to ensure fairness. Renée and Diane always offered teachers the option of having a union rep present at their evaluation if desired. These practices built a culture of trust.

## Reciprocal Accountability

Renée and Diane focused on putting kids first. They flipped the hierarchy and put families at the top. Rather than having top-down leadership, they ensured that the district was accountable to the children. That was their focus: "How can we get the kids to where they need to be, so they can become the best, well-rounded, educated child possible?"

Renée and Diane built a culture that focused on relationships and reciprocal accountability. They didn't just expect their principals to have coaches to help them improve; both Renée and Diane also had their own coaches. They set an example of humility and a willingness to learn. "We are the lead learners," they always said.

## Giving Freedom

Renée and Diane learned to be flexible with the unique needs of the individual principals they were working with. Each principal had a different approach, and Renée and Diane allowed them to use their creativity. If the principal's unique approach would be good for teachers and kids, they would let them use it. If Renée and Diane thought the approach wouldn't align with the principal's vision, they gave more direct instructions to the principal.

They differentiated between the principals who needed more skills and those who had skill sets they were choosing not to use. They always tried to help principals understand the *reason* behind their instructions. Rather than saying to principals, "This is what we need from you," they asked, "What do you need from us? What is your perspective?" They asked reflective questions and built a culture of respect.

## REFLECTIONS ON LESSONS LEARNED

As leaders, Renée and Diane share that they never need to see mistakes as regrets. Instead, they view mistakes as learning experiences for the future. We can learn from them that mistakes will help us learn something and pass on a life lesson to others.

## The Importance of Prioritization

In sharing her story, Renée wants future leaders to understand the importance of prioritization. Well into the third decade of her administrative journey, Renée had an experience that changed her life. A principal came to Renée with a concern.

"We've come back from the weekend, and I've called the police," said the principal.

Renée knew this was a principal who frequently "cried wolf," made mountains out of molehills, and treated everything as an emergency. So she took her words with a grain of salt. She asked, "Well, what happened?"

"We came back and a teacher's classroom door had 'die bi*ch' on it. We're very sure we know who did it."

When she said the name of the student, Renée got tears in her eyes. She knew he was emotionally disturbed and on medication, but he was a bright kid. The school had been working with him extensively, and Renée had a personal connection with him that she had forged during one of her many site visits. The student was interested in becoming a chef. Since Renée had a friend who was going to culinary school, she'd given the student some information and gotten him connected. Renée and the student had a unique connection.

"OK, what do you mean?" Renée asked the principal.

"When the police were called," the principal continued, "they couldn't do anything because he didn't say 'Die Mrs. Smith'. Even if we could prove it was him, they couldn't do anything. I want you to do something about it."

"I will call the police department and learn the options," Renée promised. In her heart of hearts, she thought, "It's just a statement. He didn't threaten to kill anyone." After calling the police department, she put the ball back in the principal's court.

"The police said to contact the student's counselor and talk to the mom," Renée instructed the principal. Then she let it go and didn't check in again about the topic.

A week later, over spring break, this student ordered pizza from a local establishment, restrained an employee, and raped her. When Renée found out, she was sick. The student ended up in prison, and an innocent person suffered. The reality of the situation was absolutely tragic.

"I carry a lot of responsibility that I didn't prioritize," Renée said. One of the most important things she has learned from this tragedy is that when everything is coming at you, it's absolutely crucial to prioritize what to deal with first. There's a time to give people freedom and let them grow, as Renée tried to do with this principal. But there are other times when things are so important that you have to be heavily involved.

Renée realizes in retrospect that she should have given this situation more importance. She should have been with the principal at her meeting with the student's parents. She could have been proactive to initiate a measure that could have prevented this crime.

Many top leaders face similar situations. With constant demands on their time and energy, it's difficult to know what to prioritize; however, a lack of prioritization can lead to detrimental consequences.

## The Importance of Interpersonal Skills

One of Diane's major lessons she's learned throughout her career is that she didn't learn interpersonal skills early enough. When she first became the leader of a middle school, she didn't have a clue what it would be like. For a while, she struggled with some not-so-great veteran teachers who were very set in their ways. They pushed every button that could be pushed. Her lack of interpersonal skills caused a lot of heartache. The situation became very adversarial and wasn't moving forward. Diane didn't have enough security in herself or enough tools to deal with this resistance.

Through this experience, Diane decided to get better at communication. She realized she needed to learn what it takes to establish strong interpersonal relationships, so she became very self-reflective. Diane regrets not having the interpersonal skills she needed for that situation. It was a good learning experience that helped her build up her toolbox.

During times of missteps, be willing to keep learning. Don't think you have all the answers. Be a reflective practitioner. You will learn from your mistakes. It's intended to be that way.

## REFLECTIONS ON THE BIG PICTURE

In leadership, there are so many high-intensity situations that seem insurmountable in the moment. As a younger leader, you may be dealing with very stressful situations. There doesn't seem to be any way out right now. You feel as if you're just going to break. But looking back, you will realize that some situations aren't as big of a deal as they seemed at the time. The experiences of being a seasoned leader will help you see the big picture. This is temporary. This will not last forever. It won't necessarily define your entire career. This is a bump in the road.

Diane and Renée both had their fair share of such situations that seemed critical, but weren't as life-shattering as they seemed at the time.

### Arguments Over the Closing Prayer at Graduation

Hundreds of people came to the meetings to argue over the closing prayer at graduation. People from the ministerial association called Renée and Diane bad names. There were threats. There were arguments. Parents would try to barge into the classroom and ask the administration about allowing them to pray or teach the Bible in class. Despite the intense stress of the constant threats, arguments, and intrusions, the controversy eventually subsided.

### Constantly Complaining Teachers

There always seems to be that *one* memorable staff member who files several grievances in one year. These cantankerous outliers tried to take over everything and create chaos everywhere they went. Even when a negotiator was brought in to help bring about an agreement, these people didn't want an answer. They just wanted to stir the pot, ask questions, and yell. It was difficult to figure out how to meet the minimum legal requirements to give them what they asked for without getting distracted by meeting the outliers' needs.

Renée and Diane had to constantly work to strike a balance: "We want to listen and be responsive and learn from what they have to say, but we also have to make sure the outliers don't run the show."

## Transitioning to a New School Year Calendar

Another challenging time was when Renée and Diane transitioned from a year-round calendar to a semitraditional calendar. Teachers were complaining, and the school board members themselves could not come to an agreement. Since Renée and Diane were district leaders for two districts, an elementary K–5 and a high school 9–12 district, there were two school boards with one common central office administration.

For one year, there were two entirely different bus schedules. People were arriving at different times. It was an absolute mess, as parents had students attending both districts. Diane spent many sleepless hours wondering, "How can I get these two boards to agree?"

The boards were stubborn and set in stone. Diane couldn't get the two boards to work together to make a common calendar for the sake of families and transportation. Two kids in the same family would start a week apart and have different holiday schedules. Even though this was a stressful time, it wasn't ultimately something that defined Renée and Diane.

They realized nothing was going to change until the school boards experienced for themselves how dysfunctional this plan was. This conflict only happened that year, and then, low and behold, they came to an agreement on a unified calendar.

When you're in the thick of things, these types of situations feel overwhelming. But when you look at the big picture, you realize that life will go on. These things will blow over. People will change and grow. And you will grow as well.

## REFLECTIONS ON TEAMWORK

Renée and Diane worked together as superintendent and deputy superintendent for sixteen years. They are very different people with different passions and different leadership styles. Yet they worked together with beautiful synergy. They did not allow their political, religious, or personal biases to get in the way of their career goals. Their dynamic partnership lasted many years. They may have had opposite perspectives and behind-the-scenes disagreements, but they were always unified in what they implemented. Renée and Diane reflect on the qualities that made their teamwork so effective.

## Synergy

First, they realized they couldn't do their job on their own. "We were symbiotic," they admitted. "We were two different people, but the whole was greater than the two parts." Their relationship had a synergy. Doing things together could create a greater impact than doing things on their own.

## Respect

It all boiled down to respect for each other. Diane says she learned a lot from Renée. "She was my model. That's how I got better at what I was doing. I acknowledged that she had the emotional intelligence I was trying to develop in myself, and it always helped me to observe her in action." Diane's respect for Renée helped Diane grow as a person.

Meanwhile, Renée also respected Diane. She appreciated her logical mind. She said, "I am a big-picture thinker. I can sell an idea emotionally. Diane is the strategic one. She always could find the entry point into the chaos and figure out where to start."

Renée knows she could never have done it alone. She often had nightmares that all the plates were spinning and she would drop one. Having a partner like Diane helped her keep the chaos under control. "I knew how much I respected Diane. She had a strategy," Renée reflected. The two of them recognized and respected each other's gifts and strengths.

## Trust

The word trust came up frequently in Diane's and Renée's reflections. They weren't necessarily personal friends spending much time together after work hours—"It's not like we and our husbands went out. We didn't go on vacations or anything." But they grew a great working relationship built on trust. "When you're working that many hours a week, you'd better like each other," they explain. "You'd better trust."

Diane says of Renée,

> I always knew her heart was in the right position. I trusted that. Even if I didn't quite agree with what she was doing or why, I knew it was from a good place. We've all worked with people you wouldn't be able to say that about.

Renée recognizes that because of Diane's level of success, she could have taken a superintendency position and gone anywhere she wanted to. But instead, she stayed committed to her community. Her commitment made them feel like family. It built a sense of security and trust that lasted a lifetime.

## Communication

Renée tried not to be pushy, but she knows there were times when she had to make the final decision because she was the superintendent, and Diane was the assistant superintendent. Sometimes the two of them had a different understanding. In those times, Renée used her interpersonal skills to help avoid conflict. They talked extensively about their approaches and identified areas where they needed to improve. They asked the right questions and communicated effectively.

Furthermore, they could communicate about personal needs and stresses. They knew how special their relationship was. Every superintendent is trained to "not complain down" to subordinates. They often couldn't even talk to their husbands about situations going on at work. They had to hold it all inside. But Renée and Diane had each other. They bolstered each other up when they were feeling overwhelmed.

Renée explains, "If you don't have a Diane in your life, find someone. We are much more effective as a team. Look for opportunities to build relationships. None of us can do this alone."

## Parting Reflections

Diane and Renée share their parting words of wisdom.

Diane says, "If you know that administration is what you want to do, don't be discouraged by setbacks. If you're open to on-the-job training, you can get better at it. Build some successes to start hanging your hat on. Try to find what you're best suited to do. Be willing to take risks."

Renée adds, "Administrative leadership is like a dance. There are times when you feel like a wallflower and no one is asking you to dance. Or you're asking and they're rejecting you when you do. But the bottom line is two steps forward, one step back. If you have passion and feel like your gift is to bring out the best in others, then go for it."

### YOUR TURN TO REFLECT

Now it's your turn to reflect on where you've been, where you are now, and where you're going.

Regardless of how long you've been on this journey, you have experienced the wild ride of leadership. You've traveled through the lows, the highs, and everything in between. You have flown against the wind, weathering the storms of leadership, all the while being a pilot of the aircraft called Life. In order to arrive at the destination, you have experienced travel headaches, complications, misfortunes, and bumps along the way. These are all part of the journey.

A life of leadership is full of never-ending complications, sacrifices, and heartaches at every turn. As soon as we solve one problem, there's another one waiting. There's a feeling that the work is never done. During these times, you catch yourself daydreaming about what this thing called retirement will be like: sleeping in, the travels, the cool ocean breeze. But retirement still seems like forever away.

That's why it's critically important to carve out some time to reflect on your journey. Take the time to celebrate and congratulate yourself for being a badass leader who has withstood some pretty insane challenges. If you've never done that before, now is the time to do it.

Although you aren't a rookie, you still have several years to put into your career. And you must take stock of your life *now*, before it's too late. A recent headline reads, "Americans are Retiring Later, Dying Sooner and Sicker In-Between." It is gut-wrenching to watch a seasoned leader earn their retirement stripes only to find themselves terminally ill a few years later. They have worked hard until the age of sixty plus and are finally ready to take the time to live a life of leisure. But their family members must grieve an unexpected death just a short time after the retirement celebration.

That's why it's so important for you to take the time to reflect *now*. Take a pit stop. In between flights, enjoy your layover. Take the time now to ponder the things you've read in this book.

## Ponder Ways You Need to Change

Really take stock: Do I need a better support system? Do I need more balance in my work and life? Do I need to be more proactive about anticipating danger? Am I making a difference in the lives of those around me? Do I have the resources I need to get through career disappointment without permanent damage to my mental health? Am I leaving a legacy I will one day be proud of? If you see ways you need to change, take steps today to correct your course.

## Ponder What You're Proud Of

As a leader, you know how to affirm others under your leadership care. Most likely, you say things like this every day:

"You are doing an amazing job."
"Thank you for your time on that project."
"Parents and staff are singing your praises. You are a rock star."

However, if truth be told, you know that you often tell yourself a very different story:

"Employees need more of my time."
"I need to get to the office earlier and stay later."
"I did a crappy job explaining myself to that board member."

The list of self-criticisms goes on and on. We are our own worst critics, especially when we are our own bosses. But if we are going to come out of leadership alive and invigorated, we must take extreme care of ourselves every step of the way. Speak life-giving words to yourself:

"I have come a long way, and I am continuing to grow."
"I am proud of the way I invest in my community."
"I have made a difference, and I will continue to do so."

## Ponder Ways You Can Show Appreciation

Most of all, take time to look around you and enjoy the life you have. Can you take time to treasure each pit stop along the way? Can you envision yourself as a pilot, ready to see and enjoy each country you travel to, even if the layover is only a few hours long? Can you celebrate each small victory of your staff, family, students, and colleagues? Can you show each of them how much you enjoy them?

It is possible for leaders to have a personally satisfying pre-retirement professional life, even while carrying out all the necessary leadership responsibilities and weathering the wildest storms. But you must take the time to reflect, to ponder, and to enjoy each small destination in your life. Don't get carried away with hurrying to the next rung of the career ladder and forget to enjoy the view.

No matter where you are on the journey, the destination is worth it. All the missteps along the way—career setbacks, rejection, difficulty, and hardship—are important parts of the journey that will lead you to a place of total fulfillment. Happiness is within reach at every stage of life - not just retirement.

## AIR TRAFFIC CONTROL

The journey is just as important as your destination. As you look forward to a time when you will arrive at your final destination, don't forget to look back over your career, take the time to pause, and reflect on the legacy you want to leave. Enjoy the small victories and reflect on your past, present, and future.

- Ponder the things you are proudest of. How can you build on those successes?
- Ponder the missteps you've made. How can you learn from those experiences?
- Ponder the relationships you've made along the way. How can you strengthen these relationships in the future?
- Most of all, don't forget to enjoy the journey and the small destinations along the way. One day, you'll reach your final destination. And it will be more than worth it. Let's raise our glasses to that!

**Renée, Diane, and Donya, February 2023.**
*In heartfelt memory and celebration of Diane Graziani (1948–2023).*

## NOTES

1. Pierre, "About the Pilot Who Explores." Accessed March 14, 2023, https://thepilotwhoexplores.com/about/.
2. "Play with Science and Technology." Accessed February 10, 2023, https://www.schiphol.nl/en/at-schiphol/discover/facilities/nemo.
3. "Explore What's There for You at Schiphol." Accessed February 10, 2023, https://www.schiphol.nl/en/at-schiphol.
4. "Peace and Reflection Meditation Center." Accessed February 2, 2023, https://www.schiphol.nl/en/at-schiphol/discover/facilities/meditation-centre.
5. Renée (retired superintendent), in discussion with the author, February 26, 2023.
6. Diane (retired deputy superintendent), in discussion with the author, February 26, 2023.

# Bibliography

"Airborne Wind Shear Warning Systems." *Skybrary*. March 7, 2023. https://skybrary.aero/articles/airborne-wind-shear-warning-systems.

"Aircrew." Wikipedia. Accessed September 19, 2022. https://en.wikipedia.org/wiki/Aircrew.

"Basic Instrument Reading PA28." *Flight Level*. December 15, 2022. https://flight-level.com.hk/pages/1_flight_basic.html.

Bennett, Jay. "WWII P-38 Discovered Under 300 Feet of Ice in Greenland." July 27, 2018. https://www.popularmechanics.com/flight/a22575917/wwii-p-38-discovered-under-300-feet-of-ice-in-greenland/.

Berry, Mike. "Exhaust Essentials." February 24, 2019. https://www.aviationsafetymagazine.com/aircraft/exhaust-essentials/.

Buechner, Frederick. "Wishful Thinking: A Theological ABC." *Goodreads*. March 28, 2023. https://www.goodreads.com/work/quotes/118728.

Cox, Matthew. "F-35 Pilot Killed in April Crash May Have Ignored Aircraft Instruments: Selva." June 19, 2019. https://www.military.com/daily-news/2019/06/19/f-35-pilot-killed-april-crash-may-have-ignored-aircraft-instruments-selva.html.

"Explore What's There for You at Schiphol." February 10, 2023. https://www.schiphol.nl/en/at-schiphol.

FAA. *Weight and Balance Handbook*. Newcastle, WA: Aviation Supplies & Academics, Inc., 2016. Accessed on US Department of Transportation. November 30, 2021. https://www.faa.gov/regulations_policies/handbooks_manuals/aviation/media/faa-h-8083-1.pdf.

Given, Molly. "How Daniel Seddiqui was Able to 'Piece Together America.'" December 15, 2022. https://metrophiladelphia.com/daniel-seddiqui-piece-together-america/.

"Glacier Girl." Wikipedia. February 1, 2023. https://en.wikipedia.org/wiki/Glacier_Girl.

"How Does an Aircraft Exhaust System Affect Engine Performance?" *Acorn Welding*. May 26, 2020. https://www.acornwelding.com/blog/post/aircraft-exhaust-system-affect-engine-performance/.

"How Much of a Pilot's Training Is Emergency Landing Practices?" March 20, 2017. https://slate.com/human-interest/2017/03/how-much-of-a-pilots-training-is-emergency-landing-practices.html.

Koenig, David. "How 9/11 Changed Air Travel: More Security, Less Privacy." September 6, 2021. https://apnews.com/article/how-sept-11-changed-flying-1ce4dc4282fb47a34c0b61ae09a024f4.

Lee, Morgan. "20 Cuban Pastors and Spouses Killed in Plane Crash." *Christianity Today*. May 21, 2018. https://www.christianitytoday.com/news/2018/may/cuba-pastors-spouses-killed-in-havana-plane-crash-nazarene.html.

Manzoni, Matthieu, and Lucy Luo. "4 Innovative Business Pivots in the Age of the Pandemic." December 17, 2020. https://www.strategyzer.com/blog/4-innovative-business-pivots-in-the-age-of-the-pandemic.

"NTSB: Improper Loading Caused Challenger Jet Crash." *Aviation Software Solutions*. November 30, 2022. https://www.eflite.com/news/aircraft_weight_balance_crash_1.php.

"Number of Aircraft Hijackings in the Aviation Industry Worldwide from 1990 to 2021." *Statista*. April 12, 2022. https://www.statista.com/statistics/1240246/aircraft-hijackings-worldwide/.

Page, Charlie. "A Passenger's Guide to Turbulence." May 4, 2019. https://thepointsguy.com/guide/pax-guide-to-turbulence/.

Page, Charlie. "How the Atmosphere and Winds Affect Your Flight." June 23, 2019. https://thepointsguy.com/news/how-atmosphere-winds-affect-your-flight/.

"Peace and Reflection Meditation Center." February 2, 2023. https://www.schiphol.nl/en/at-schiphol/discover/facilities/meditation-centre.

Pierre. "About the Pilot Who Explores." *The Pilot Who Explores*. March 14, 2023. https://thepilotwhoexplores.com/about.

"Plane Crash Cleanup." *S&R Environmental*. March 10, 2023. https://www.srrenviro.com/sub-services/plane-crash-cleanup/.

"Play with Science and Technology." February 10, 2023. https://www.schiphol.nl/en/at-schiphol/discover/facilities/nemo.

Ritchie, Hannah, Joe Hassell, Edouard Mathieu, Cameron Appel, and Max Rose. "Terrorism." October 2022. https://ourworldindata.org/terrorism#airline-hijackings.

Schaper, David. "It Was Shoes On, No Boarding Pass or ID. But Airport Security Forever Changed On 9/11." September 10, 2021. https://www.npr.org/2021/09/10/1035131619/911-travel-timeline-tsa.

Sengupta, Ahona. "'Weight and Balance' Errors Caused Deadly Cuba Air Crash That Killed 112 People." May 17, 2019. https://www.news18.com/news/world/weight-and-balance-errors-caused-deadly-cuba-air-crash-that-killed-112-people-2144243.html.

Silitch, Mary F. "Out-of-limit cg Might have Led to TEB Crash." *AINonline*. October 31, 2006. https://www.ainonline.com/aviation-news/aviation-international-news/2006-10-31/out-limit-cg-might-have-led-teb-crash.

"The Lost Squadron." PBS. February 1, 2023. https://www.myarkansaspbs.org/programs/lost_squadron.

"The Six Pack: Basic Flight Instruments." *Pilot Institute.* December 6, 2021. https://pilotinstitute.com/six-pack-instruments/.

"Warning Systems." *The Boeing 737 Technical Site.* March 7, 2023. http://www.b737.org.uk/warningsystems.htm.

Waters, Shonna, PhD. "How to Tap into Heart and Soul to Lead with More Charisma." November 30, 2021. https://www.nytimes.com/1988/08/04/us/world-war-ii-planes-found-in-greenland-in-ice-260-feet-deep.html.

"What Is an Aircraft Exhaust System Analysis?" *Acorn Welding.* December 15, 2022. https://www.acornwelding.com/blog/post/what-aircraft-exhaust-system-analysis/.

"World War II Planes Found in Greenland in Ice 260 Feet Deep." August 4, 1988. https://www.nytimes.com/1988/08/04/us/world-war-ii-planes-found-in-greenland-in-ice-260-feet-deep.html.

# About the Author

**Dr. Donya Ball** is a leader, author, and national speaker. She currently serves as a superintendent of schools in California. She has been a change-maker in public education for over two decades. Dr. Ball is a professor of both educational administration and teacher education and is passionate about studying, writing, and speaking about overcoming leadership hardships. She published her first book of the leadership series, *Adjusting the Sails: Weathering the Storms of Administrative Leadership*, in 2022, followed by *Against the Wind: Leadership at 36,000 Feet*. Prior to her superintendency and work in higher education, Dr. Ball was a teacher in elementary and middle schools and a reading specialist. She then served as an assistant principal, principal, and assistant superintendent.

www.ingramcontent.com/pod-product-compliance
Lightning Source LLC
Chambersburg PA
CBHW030140240426
43672CB00005B/202